Fun with Foods
A Recipe For Math + Science

Authors

Albert M. Alfving   Rose Lee Patron

C. Lloyd Eitzen   Helen Holve

Joanne Hyman   Philip Nelson

Illustrator

Sheryl Mercier

Editors

Karen Buffington   Larry Ecklund

Shery Mercier   Arthur Wiebe

AIMS Education Foundation •Fresno, California

AIMS (Activities Integrating Mathematics and Science) began in 1981 with a grant from the National Science Foundation. The non-profit AIMS Education Foundation publishes hands-on instructional materials (books and the monthly AIMS Newsletter) that integrate curricular disciplines such as mathematics, science, language arts, and social studies. The Foundation sponsors a national program of professional development through which educators may gain both an understanding of the AIMS philosophy and expertise in teaching by integrated, hands-on methods.

ISBN 1-881431-07-X

Printed in the United States of America

Table of Contents

Fun with Foods
A Recipe For Math + Science

As one of man's primary needs, food has been referred to in literature, music legends and rhymes. From *Pat-a-Cake* to *Little Tommy Tucker*, from *Jack Sprat* to *Little Jack Horner*, food enters a child's education at the very early years. We sing about it, celebrate it, and suffer because we consume too much of it. It is only fitting, therefore, that food also play an important role in education through the integration of basic concepts in mathematics and science.

This book shows how to teach and reinforce skills and processes in math and science through the fun and fantasy of food. The wonderment and curiosity that is aroused in working and playing with foods is the beginning of many discoveries along a student's path to knowledge.

Value may be found in everything from peeling an orange and estimating the number of sections, to figuring out the fractional part of the vegetables in your bowl of *Fraction Soup*.

The mathematics-science center becomes a laboratory because opportunities abound on the spot when children cook or work with foods. Even the youngest student is ready to consider the concept of emulsions when making homemade mayonnaise; the older student's curiosity might demand the more sophisticated explanations that are offered in *The Red C* or *Popcorn Comparisons*.

The materials and equipment you need for most of the investigations can be found in the kitchen, the corner market, or the school classroom.

Learning through these investigations using foods can be fun, educational, sensual, constructive, and delightful. However, the well-prepared teacher is still the most important ingredient in a successful classroom environment. Take your time in reading these investigations and preparing them so that you may enjoy a rewarding experience with your students.

Index to Skills

I HEAR, AND I FORGET

I SEE, AND I REMEMBER

I DO, AND I UNDERSTAND

–Chinese Proverb

Waste Not Want Not !

I. Topic Area
Determining the usable parts of food by weight.

II. Introductory Statement
In this activity the students will discover the relationship between the usable parts of foods and their protective coverings.

III. Math Skills
a. Graphing
b. Finding percent
c. Averaging

Science Processes
a. Recording data
b. Estimating
c. Measuring

IV. Materials
Fruits that are easy to peel such as:

Oranges	Bananas
Lemons	Avocados

Other materials:

Scales (at least three)	Paring knife
Masses (metric)	
Paper plates	

V. Key Questions
"Would you eat a banana before you peel it? What about an orange? Can you use the peels for anything?"

VI. Background Information
In order to determine the percent of fruit that is edible, divide the edible mass by the total mass (weight).

VII. Management Suggestions
1. Demonstrate the use of the measuring instrument.
2. Demonstrate metric measurements.
3. Have students be responsible for bringing the fruit.
4. Allot about 40 minutes for the investigation.

Hint: Remind students not to use the mouth to begin peeling fruit.

VIII. Procedure
1. Have students estimate the mass (weight) of each fruit. Record.
2. Have students estimate the number of sections, if applicable.
3. Mass (weigh) the fruit. Record.
4. Estimate the mass of fruit without the peel. Record.
5. Mass the peeled fruit. Record.
6. To check the data, students may also mass the peels.

IX. What the Students Will Do
The students will discover how much of a fruit is edible, and that some fruits have more waste than others.

X. Discussion
1. What purpose does the peel play?
2. Do the same fruits have the same amount of sections?
3. What is a better buy as far as edible fruit is concerned?
4. Is the peel usable?

XI. Extension
1. This same experiment may be done with nuts with shells such as those indicated in "In a Nutshell."
2. Make a fruit salad.
3. Determine the percentage of juice from citrus fruits.
4. Prepare this Banana Surprise:
   Ingredients: 1 banana
                    2 tablespoons peanut butter
   Procedure:
   a. Slice the peeled banana in half lengthwise.
   b. Spread one half of the banana with the peanut butter.
   c. Put the other half of the banana on top.
5. Make fruit juice from the lemons, oranges, or grapefruits.

_____ name

Waste Not Want Not!

What part of a fruit is edible?

Record all data in grams (g)

Kind of Fruit	Total Weight		Weight of Peeling		Weight of Edible Part		Number of Sections		Per Cent Edible %	Per Cent Waste %
	EST.	ACTUAL	EST.	ACTUAL	EST.	ACTUAL	EST.	ACTUAL		
A.										
B.										
C.										
D.										
E.										
Total										
Average										

Per Cent of Edible Fruit

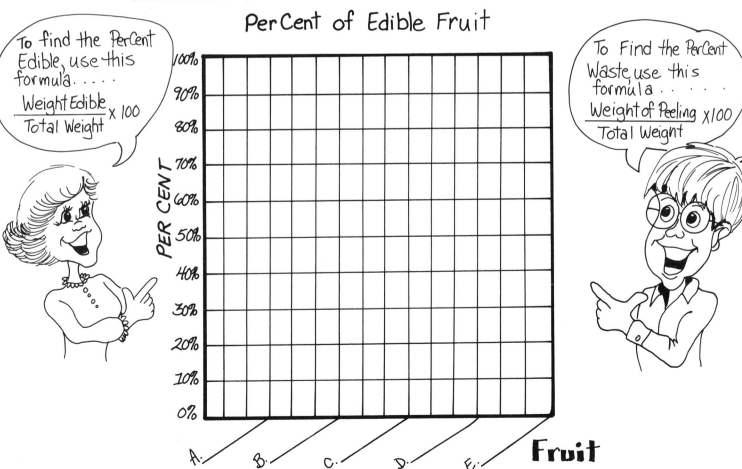

To find the Per Cent Edible, use this formula . . . . .
$$\frac{\text{Weight Edible}}{\text{Total Weight}} \times 100$$

To Find the Per Cent Waste, use this formula . . . . .
$$\frac{\text{Weight of Peeling}}{\text{Total Weight}} \times 100$$

PER CENT

100%
90%
80%
70%
60%
50%
40%
30%
20%
10%
0%

A. ___ B. ___ C. ___ D. ___ E. ___ **Fruit**

In A Nutshell

I. **Topic Area**

Determining the usable parts of nuts by weight.

II. **Introductory Statement**

In this activity the students will discover the usable parts of nuts and their protective coverings.

III. **Math Skills**
   a. Graphing
   b. Finding percent
   c. Averaging

Science Processes
   a. Recording data
   b. Estimating
   c. Measuring

IV. **Materials**

Any nuts with shells such as peanuts, walnuts, pecans, almonds, etc.
Balances (at least three)
Metric masses
Nutcrackers
Paper plates

V. **Key Questions**

"Why do you remove the shells before you eat nuts?"
"Why do nuts have shells?"
"Of which is there more: edible food or waste?"

VI. **Background Information**

In order to determine the percent of each nut that is edible, divide the edible mass by the total mass.

VII. **Management Suggestions**
   1. Demonstrate the use of the measuring instrument(s).
   2. Demonstrate and review metric measurement.

3. Allot approximately 40 minutes for the investigation.

VIII. **Procedure**
   1. Divide the class into small groups of five or six.
   2. Have a variety of nuts available for each group.
   3. Estimate the total mass of each kind of nut and record.
   4. Mass each kind of nut and record.
   5. Estimate the mass of each kind of shelled nuts (without shells). Record.
   6. Remove the shells and mass the nuts without the shells and record.
   7. To check their data, students may also mass the shells.

IX. **What the Students Will Do**

The students will discover and compare the edible portions of different types of nuts.

X. **Discussion**
   1. What purpose does the shell play?
   2. Which is a better buy as far as the edible portion of the nut is concerned?
   3. Is the shell usable?

XI. **Extension**
   1. Use this investigation in conjunction with "Waste Not, Want Not."
   2. Prepare nut butter by grinding the nuts in a flour mill, grinder, or blender.

In A Nutshell

NAME _____

KIND OF NUTS	TOTAL WEIGHT		WEIGHT OF SHELL		WEIGHT OF EDIBLE PART		Number of SECTIONS		PERCENT EDIBLE	PERCENT WASTE
	ESTIMATE	ACTUAL	EST.	ACT.	EST.	ACT.	EST.	ACT.		
A.										
B.										
C.										
D.										
E.										
Total										
Average										

FORMULAS

Per Cent Edible = $\dfrac{\text{Weight of Edible Part}}{\text{Total Weight}} \times 100$

Per Cent Waste = $\dfrac{\text{Weight of Shell}}{\text{TOTAL Weight}} \times 100$

PER CENT EDIBLE OF NUTS

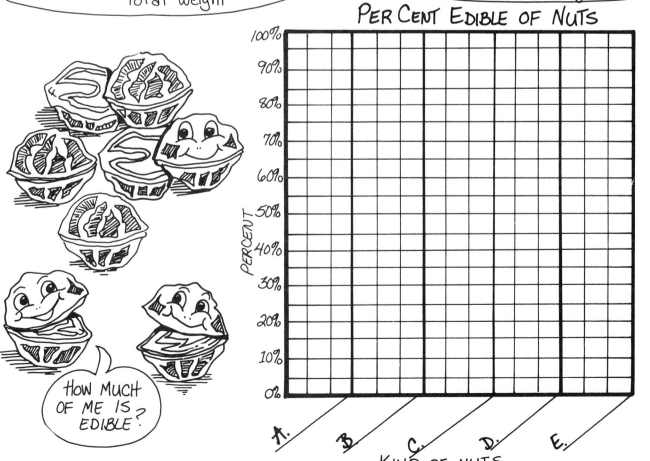

HOW MUCH OF ME IS EDIBLE?

KIND OF NUTS

A.   B.   C.   D.   E.

It's A-Peeling

I. Topic Area
Determining the edible part of an orange by volume.

II. Introductory Statement
Students will discover the ratio between the edible volume of an orange and its protective covering.

III. Math Skills
a. Measuring
b. Estimating
c. Subtracting
d. Averaging
e. Finding percent
f. Graphing

Science Processes
a. Predicting
b. Observing
c. Recording data
d. Interpreting data

IV. Materials
1 liter cube or graduated beaker
100 ml graduated cylinder
5 oranges per group (different sizes if possible)
Paper towels
Sharp knife
Paper plates
Large bowl
Container for water, such as a large pitcher
Ball of clay
Marble
Golf ball

V. Key Question
"What percent of this orange do you eat? What percent is thrown away?"

VI. Background Information
1. Volume is the amount of space an object occupies.
2. The unpeeled orange will float and the peeled orange will sink because the peeling is less dense than the pulp of the fruit.
3. To determine the percent of edible fruit, divide the edible volume by the total volume.
4. The formula for volume of a sphere is $V = 4/3\pi r^2$.
5. 1 milliliter equals 1 cubic centimeter. $1\ ml = 1\ cm^3$.

VII. Management Suggestions
1. The best results are obtained with different size oranges, but they are not always easy to obtain. You might try having students bring the fruit.
2. Students should practice estimating volume (using objects such as a golf ball, marble (use 100 ml graduated cylinder), or clay (determine volume as a ball, knead it and change its shape—ask "Will the volume be the same?"—Yes!)
3. This investigation can be done with the whole class or as a small group activity.

IX. What the Students Will Do
1. Place oranges on 5 plates marked A, B, C, D, E.
2. Estimate the volume of unpeeled orange. Record on chart.
3. Pour 500 ml water into beaker or liter cube.
4. Submerse object in water, using paper clip or pencil to completely submerge.
5. Estimate number of segments and record.
6. Peel orange, estimate volume of fruit and number of segments. Record.
7. Measure volume of peeled orange. Record.
8. Continue with other four oranges. Be sure that the beginning level of water is 500 ml.
9. Count segments. Record.
10. Complete chart and graph.
11. Compute percent.

X. Discussion
1. The children will discover that approximately ⅔ of an orange is edible. The larger the orange, the more segments, and usually (depending on the time of season) the more waste.
2. What size orange do you feel is a better buy?
3. Some students may ask and others may know why the whole orange floats (the peeling is less dense). This may lead to a discussion on density (see extension).

XI. Extension
1. You can measure density by weighing the whole orange, the peeled orange, and the peeling of the orange. Use the formula $D = \frac{m}{v}$. If weighing to compute density, do this before submerging in water.
2. If oranges are uniformly round, older students can compute the volume by using the formula $V = 4/3\pi r^2$.
3. Make a fruit salad using the peeled oranges.
4. Make Candied Orange Peel.
5. This is a good follow-up for "Big Banana Peel," (Book 1) and can be done in conjunction with "Waste Not, Want Not."

Recipe—Candied Orange Peel
• Prepare orange peel in thin strips, removing all the white part inside the skin. • Cover the strips with boiling water and let stand for 1 hour. • Pour off the water and boil in fresh water for 20 minutes. • Prepare a heavy syrup of 2 cups sugar and 1 cup water. • Boil the peel in the syrup until tender and then remove from the syrup. • Cool and sprinkle with granulated sugar.

It's A-Peeling

	TOTAL VOLUME IN MILLIMETERS		EDIBLE VOLUME IN MILLIMETERS		VOLUME OF PEELING IN ml	NUMBER OF SECTIONS		PERCENT EDIBLE %	PERCENT WASTE %
	ESTIMATE	ACTUAL	ESTIMATE	ACTUAL		ESTIMATE	ACTUAL		
A.									
B.									
C.									
D.									
E.									
Total									
Average									

ORANGES

FORMULA : PERCENT EDIBLE % = $\dfrac{\text{EDIBLE VOLUME}}{\text{TOTAL VOLUME}} \times 100$

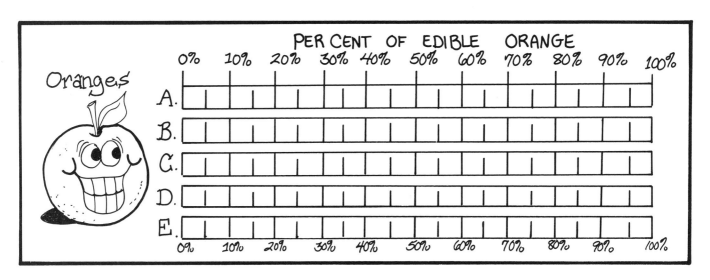

#1 POPCORN COMPARISON

I. **Topic Area**
Volume and comparison of brands of popcorn.

II. **Introductory Statement**
Students will discover that different brands of popcorn yield different volumes of popped corn, and will try to generalize as to why some popcorn will produce greater volume.

III. **Math Skills**
a. Measuring
b. Computing
c. Counting
d. Estimating

Science Processes
a. Observing
b. Sequencing
c. Recording data
d. Interpreting data
e. Forming hypotheses

IV. **Materials**
Two brands of popcorn
Popcorn popper
Oil
Large bowls
Metric measuring cups, spoons or beakers
Liter cube or liter pitcher
Paper towels

V. **Key Question**
"Will different brands of popcorn yield different volumes when they are popped under the same conditions?"

VI. **Background Information**
It is very important that each measurement be made very carefully. This is the time to explain accuracy of measurements. The meniscus of the oil measurement should be used to determine the quantity of oil when beakers are used.

It is faster as well as more sanitary to count kernels prior to the popping time. This allows an activity for the students who are not involved with the actual preparation and cooking.

VII. **Management Suggestions**
1. Divide the class into 2 teams, one for each brand of popcorn. Each team is to consist of committees for counting, measurement, food preparation, and clean-up.
2. A chalkboard or overhead transparency is essential to keep all students posted on the progress of the experiment as well as giving them the opportunity of compiling their own data as both teams continue the investigations.
3. Allow 2 class periods, one for preparation of the popcorn and filling in the data sheet, and the second for graphing results, discussing the outcomes, and computing the percentage of edible corn.

VIII. **Procedure**
1. Observe the popping of a single kernel of popcorn from brand A and brand B.

2. Compare the results. Are the sequences the same? Does one brand of popcorn pop faster than the other? Is one kernel different in any way? Based on what you have seen, what results would you predict for this investigation?
3. Record your predictions.
4. Assign committee tasks. Measure oil and popcorn, count kernels. Estimate the volume of the popped corn.
5. Pop the popcorn.
6. Separate the duds (those kernels which did not open) from the fluffy popcorn. Count and record the duds.
7. Subtract the number of duds from the number of kernels in the sample.
8. Measure the popcorn in the liter cube. Decimals can be used for students who are able to multiply and divide decimals.
9. Complete the investigation by repeating steps 4-8 with the other samples. Students should report results to the leader so that the results can be posted on a chalkboard or overhead.
10. Using equal ratios, compute the percentage of duds. Subtract the percentage of duds from 100% to find the percentage of edible popcorn.
11. Compare the recorded data and reach hypothesis.

IX. **What the Students Will Do**
The students can conduct this project from beginning to end. Teacher supervision will take the form of guidance and leading the discussion after all the data has been collected.

X. **Discussion Questions**
1. Do both brands of popcorn yield equal volumes? Why or why not?
2. Which brand is a better buy? Why?
3. If we tried other brands, what would be the results?
4. Can you predict how much popcorn you will get from a measure of popcorn?
5. Which popcorn would you purchase?

XI. **Extension**
1. See the Introductory Book, page 21, for a popcorn investigation in developing a ratio for popping corn.
2. Compare the weight before and after popping.
3. Compute the percentage increase of volume from the dry state to the popped.
4. Compare the price of popcorn by volume to other snack foods.
5. Send your questions to the manufacturer. They have been known to respond to the class and individual students.
6. Construct bar graph comparisons using as many brands of popcorn as you can find locally. One sample of the same measurement would be adequate for this type of comparison. Test for volume or for flavor.

#1 POPCORN COMPARISON

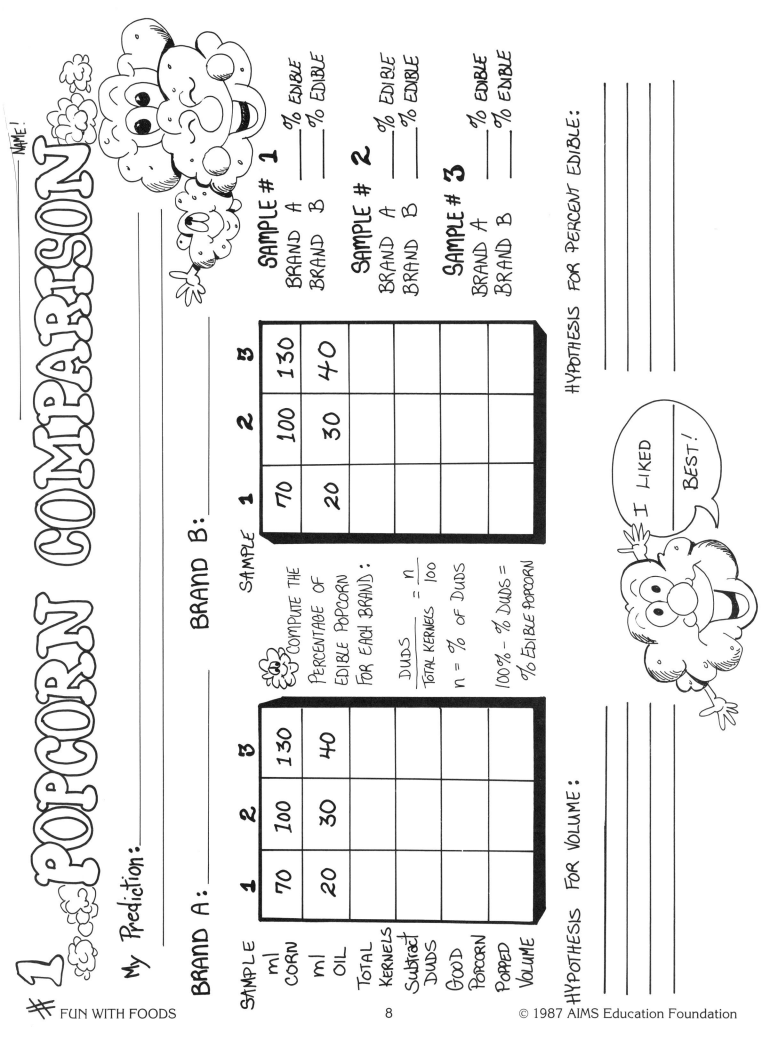

My Prediction: _____

BRAND A: _____

BRAND B: _____

BRAND A

SAMPLE	1	2	3
ml CORN	70	100	130
ml OIL	20	30	40
TOTAL KERNELS			
Subtract DUDS			
GOOD POPCORN			
POPPED VOLUME			

BRAND B

SAMPLE	1	2	3
ml CORN	70	100	130
ml OIL	20	30	40

Compute the Percentage of Edible Popcorn for each Brand:

$$\frac{DUDS}{TOTAL\ KERNELS} = \frac{n}{100}$$

n = % of DUDS

100% - % DUDS = % Edible Popcorn

SAMPLE # 1
BRAND A _____ % EDIBLE
BRAND B _____ % EDIBLE

SAMPLE # 2
BRAND A _____ % EDIBLE
BRAND B _____ % EDIBLE

SAMPLE # 3
BRAND A _____ % EDIBLE
BRAND B _____ % EDIBLE

HYPOTHESIS FOR VOLUME: _____

HYPOTHESIS FOR PERCENT EDIBLE: _____

I LIKED _____ BEST!

#2 POPCORN COMPARISON

I. Topic Area
Volume and comparison of the results by changing the variables prior to popping popcorn.

II. Introductory Statement
Students will discover which variables affect the volume of popped corn.

III. Math Skills
a. Measuring
b. Estimating
c. Logical thinking

Science Processes
a. Recording data
b. Controlling variables
c. Interpreting data
d. Hypothesizing

IV. Materials
Popcorn
Popcorn popper
Oil
Large bowls
Liter cube or liter pitcher

Metric measuring spoons or milliliter graduated cylinders
Paper Towels

V. Key Question
"Will changing the variables affect the volume of popped corn?"

VI. Background Information
Moisture content of the popcorn kernel will have a bearing on the volume of the popped corn. This moisture, when quickly heated, causes pressure on the seed coat, causing the seed coat to crack and force the contents to expand as the steam is released.

The type of heat as well as the temperature have direct influences on the results of this experiment. Two poppers can be used, but to insure accurate results your class may want to repeat the experiment after the committees exchange poppers.

VII. Management Suggestions
1. Advance preparation by the teacher or a student of the popcorn with the variable conditions should be done the day prior to the investigation.
2. Decide which variables your class will use. Actual preparation time should not exceed 15 minutes.
3. Before the onset of the investigation, student committees should be assigned popping and clean-up responsibilities.

4. A chalkboard, chart, or overhead transparency of the worksheet is helpful to students in completing the data sheet.
5. Under adult supervision all students can participate in this investigation. Estimated volumes can be recorded while the popping committee pops the corn. Predictions as to possible results can also be discussed.
6. During the time one batch of corn has been popped and the next batch is being prepared, discussion of the first results as well as the possible results of the next variables can be discussed.

VIII. Procedures
1. Discuss the scientific processes of controlling variables to determine optimum reliable results. In this investigation maximum volume is the desired solution.
2. Explain how each sample was prepared for the variables.
3. Pop the popcorn using the recipe on the student sheet (130 m. popcorn, 40 ml oil). Measure the popcorn by using liter cube or liter pitcher. Enter the volume in the appropriate box.
4. Samples which were soaked must be drained and patted dry before following the above recipe.
5. Record, graph, and discuss the results.

X. Discussion Questions
1. Which variables cause the largest yield? Why?
2. Which variables cause the lowest yields? Why?
3. How is the quality of popcorn affected by the variables?
4. Were you able to estimate the volumes accurately? Why or why not?
5. Did the results surprise you? How?

XI. Extension
1. Have a taste survey by comparing the taste of the results of popping corn under the various variables.
2. Compute the cost per serving of the different volumes. Why is a greater volume desirable?
3. Conduct a comparison study of brands using the same variables.

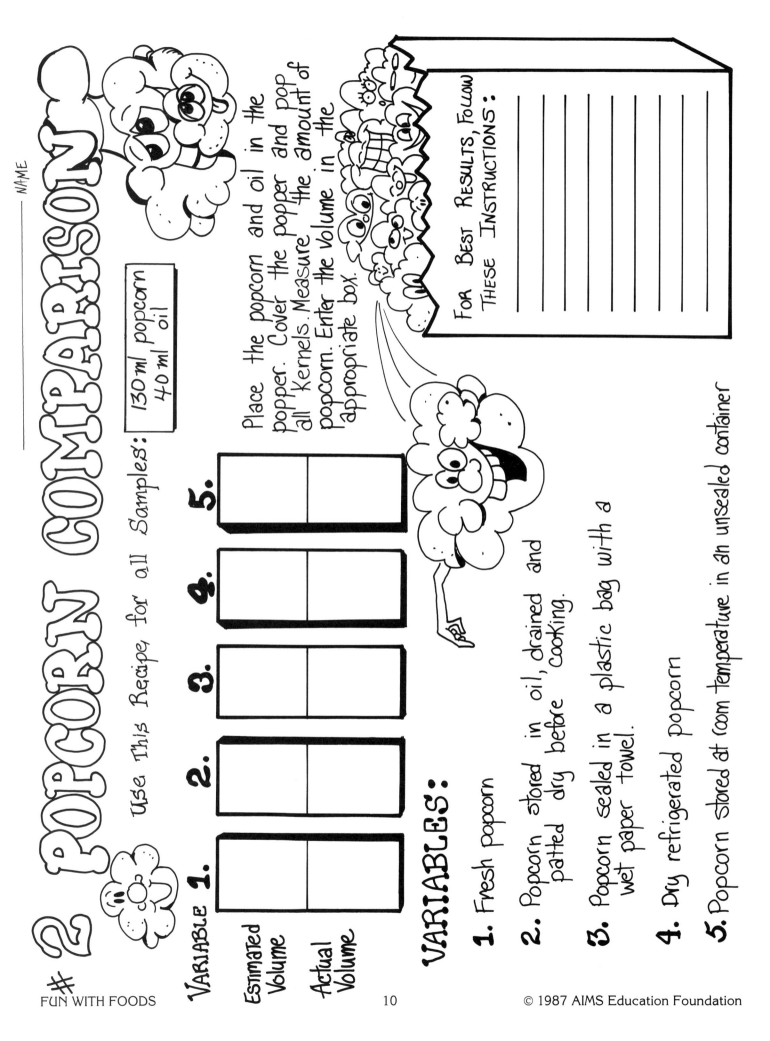

#2 POPCORN COMPARISON

NAME —

Use This Recipe for all Samples:

| 130ml popcorn |
| 40 ml oil |

For Best Results, Follow These Instructions:

Place the popcorn and oil in the popper. Cover the popper and pop all kernels. Measure the amount of popcorn. Enter the volume in the appropriate box.

VARIABLE **1.** **2.** **3.** **4.** **5.**

Estimated Volume

Actual Volume

VARIABLES:

1. Fresh popcorn

2. Popcorn stored in oil, drained and patted dry before cooking.

3. Popcorn sealed in a plastic bag with a wet paper towel.

4. Dry refrigerated popcorn

5. Popcorn stored at room temperature in an unsealed container

FUN WITH FOODS   10   © 1987 AIMS Education Foundation

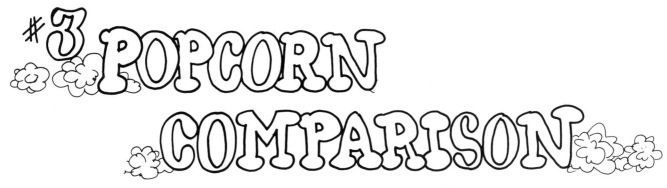

#3 POPCORN COMPARISON

I. Topic Area
Expansion formula development for popcorn using various forms of measurement.

II. Introductory Statement
Students will make choices applying scientific principles of experimentation in conducting their own investigations. Metric or standard measurement can be selected as well as solving for volume, area, or linear measure of popcorn.

III. Math Skills
a. Measuring
b. Computing
c. Counting
d. Developing a formula

Science Processes
a. Observing
b. Controlling
c. Recording data
d. Interpreting data

IV. Materials
Popcorn and popcorn popper
Oil
Large bowls
Metric and/or standard measuring cups, spoons, cubes, quart jars, rulers
Paper cut into 10 cm x 30 cm or 3 inch x 12 inch lengths
Square cm grids, square inch grids
Paper towels

V. Key Question
"Is there a formula for estimating the amount of popcorn needed?"

VI. Background Information
Basic popcorn information is listed with Popcorn Comparisons 1 and 2. This investigation can be used for independent study at home or school. If a pattern develops with the amount of corn that is used, the students may be able to arrive at their own formula for popcorn expansion.

VII. Management Suggestions
1. Students participating in the independent study should make a presentation to the class.
2. As an alternate method, students can do the investigation in class, present the data, and have the other students participate in developing the formula.
3. As a class project, let the students decide how the investigation should be set up. Let them choose the form of measurements, organize themselves, and select the variables.
4. See Book 1, *Introductory Investigations*, page 21, for the development of a formula for volume.
5. Fold paper lengthwise for ease of linear measure. See diagram.

VIII. Procedures
1. In using the data sheet, decide which form the investigation will take.
2. What form of measurement will be used? Circle the correct form.
3. How will you control the variables?
4. At this point, each individual or a group can conduct the investigation and complete the data sheet.

X. Discussion Questions
1. Were the measurements effective?
2. How many variables were tested?
3. Which method of measurement was the most reliable? Why?
4. Is there a relationship between unpopped kernels and popped popcorn?
5. How will the pattern that evolves help us to construct a formula?

XI. Extension
1. How much popcorn is needed to cover a table surface?
2. How much popcorn would it take to make a chain a mile long?
3. How much popcorn is needed for a cubic meter or a cubic yard?
4. Weigh popcorn for a given measurement before and after popping.

#3 POPCORN COMPARISON

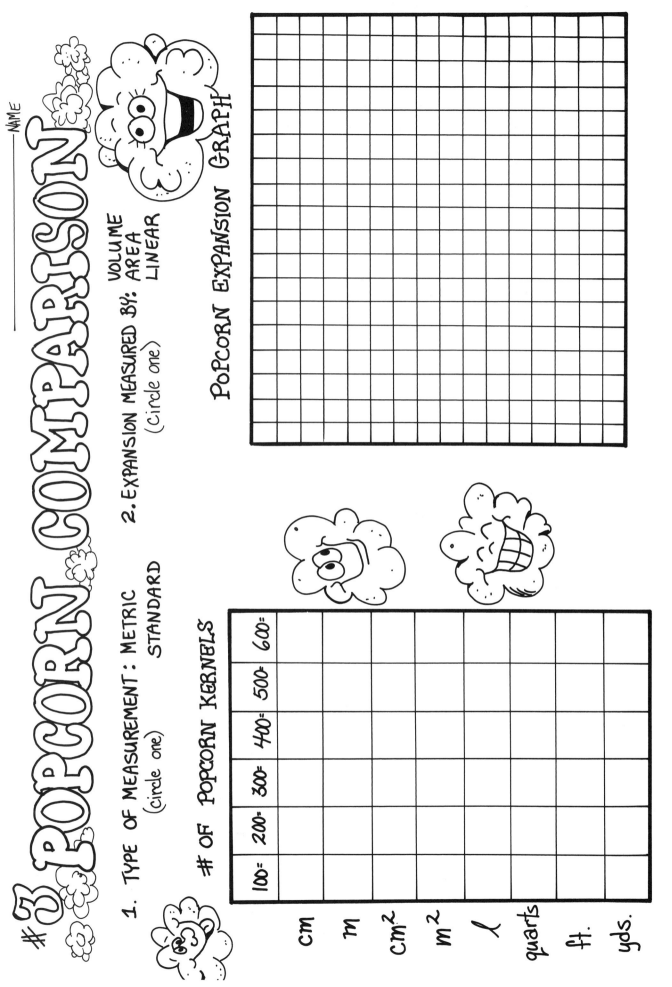

NAME _____

1. TYPE OF MEASUREMENT: METRIC   STANDARD
   (circle one)

2. EXPANSION MEASURED BY: VOLUME
   (circle one)   AREA
                            LINEAR

POPCORN EXPANSION GRAPH

OF POPCORN KERNELS

	100=	200=	300=	400=	500=	600=
cm						
m						
cm²						
m²						
ℓ						
quarts						
ft.						
yds.						

Snack Attack

I. Topic Area
Consumer Economics

II. Introductory Statement
The students will classify, identify, and measure the quantity of each ingredient to reconstruct a homemade recipe. The investigation will result in comparisons of taste, cost, and appearance of prepackaged snack mixes to homemade products.

III. Math Skills
a. Sorting
b. Problem Solving
c. Estimating
d. Finding percent

Science Processes
a. Observing
b. Classifying
c. Recording data
d. Interpreting data
e. Predicting

IV. Materials
Prepackaged snack mix, containing any or all of the following ingredients: cereal, pretzels, nuts, raisins, and dried fruit.
Materials for homemade mix per recipes
Balance scale and weights

V. Key Question
"Are homemade snack mixtures better and less expensive than prepackaged snack mixtures?"

VI. Background Information
The type of packaging has a direct bearing on the cost of the product. Commercial preparation of snack products could increase the cost.

VII. Management Suggestions
1. Depending on grade, choose the type of mixture with appropriate number of components.
   Simplest—Honey Cracker Jacks
             Party Snack Mix
   Hardest —Trail Mix
2. This is a small or whole group activity.
3. Time limit—approximately 2 one-hour sessions.

VIII. Procedure
Session I
1. Choose appropriate mix to be used.
2. Prepare homemade recipe.
3. Conduct a taste test, comparing the prepackaged and homemade mixtures.
4. Divide the class into convenient size working groups (5 or 6).
5. Estimate quantities before sorting.
6. Sort each category.
7. Estimate quantities after sorting.
8. Weigh each category.
9. Graph quantity results on bar graph.

Session II
1. Calculate percentages and graph on circle graph.
2. Calculate the cost of individual categories.
3. Calculate the cost of individual categories using homemade mixture.
4. Draw your final conclusions.

X. Discussion
1. Which mixture is better? How?
2. How accurate was your estimating?
3. Which category cost the most?
4. What other mixtures could be used for this experiment?
5. Which costs less, prepackaged or homemade? Why?

XI. Extension
1. Students could develop more economical mixtures of their own.
2. Other mixes could be used to see if similar results will occur.
3. Students could also do comparisons of prepackaged mixtures, like macaroni and cheese and T.V. dinners.

RECIPES

Cruncho Mix
Mix 4 C. crunchy cereal (any combination)
      1 C. peanuts or mixed nuts
      1 C. pretzel sticks
      1 C. seasoned croutons
Combine 1 C. salad oil or 6 Tbsp. melted butter
      2 tsp. Worcestershire Sauce
      1/4 tsp. garlic powder

In a large shallow pan, coat crunchy ingredients with the combined oil and seasoning. Heat in oven at 250 degrees for 45 minutes, stirring every 15 minutes. Spread on absorbent paper to cool.
Taken from: *The Taming of the C.A.N.D.Y. Monster* by Vicky Lansky, Published by Meadowbrook Press.

Honey "Cracker Jacks"
1/2 C. (6 Tbsp) honey
1/4 C. butter or margarine
  6 C. popped corn
  1 C. shelled peanuts

Heat honey and shortening in a saucepan until blended. Cool. Pour over popcorn which has been mixed with peanuts, stirring as you pour. When well-coated, spread on a pan in a single layer. Bake 350° 5-10 minutes or until crisp, stirring several times. The difference between crisp (not brown) and burnt can be a matter of minutes. Package in plastic bags and twist ties. If you want it to be mistaken for the "real thing" add a small toy. Variation: Food coloring added to honey gives a festive appearance.
Taken from: *The Taming of the C.A.N.D.Y. Monster*, by Vicky Lansky, Published by Meadowbrook Press.

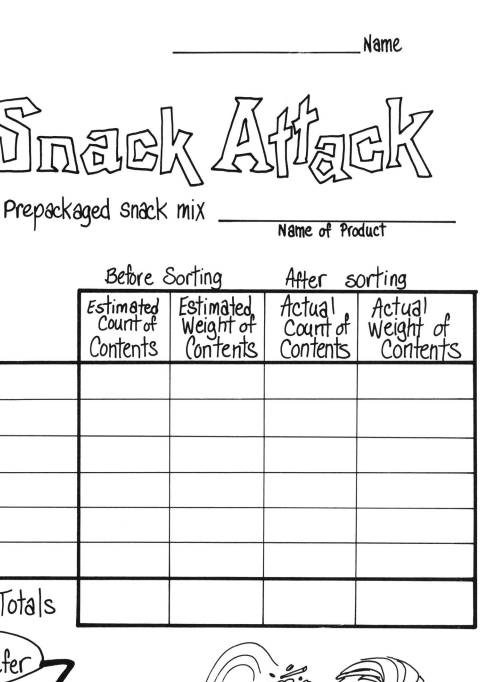

_____ Name

Snack Attack

Prepackaged snack mix _____
Name of Product

Ingredients	Before Sorting		After sorting	
	Estimated Count of Contents	Estimated Weight of Contents	Actual Count of Contents	Actual Weight of Contents
1.				
2.				
3.				
4.				
5.				
6.				
Totals				

I Prefer

Homemade	
Packaged	

I liked _____ because _____

_____

_____

_____

Snack Attack

☆ Pre-packaged: _____
Name

Total Weight _____
Price _____
Price per Serving _____

Ingredients	Net Count	Net Weight
1.		
2.		
3.		
4.		
5.		
6.		
Totals		

$$Cost = \frac{Net\ Weight}{Package\ Weight} \times Package\ Price$$

☆ Homemade: _____
Name

Total Weight _____
Price _____
Price per serving _____

Ingredients	Net Count	Net Weight	Price
1.			
2.			
3.			
4.			
5.			
6.			
Totals			

_____ Class

Snack Attack
Which tastes best?

Student Name	Purchased	Homemade
1.		
2.		
3.		
4.		
5.		
6.		
7.		
8.		
9.		
10.		
11.		
12.		
13.		
14.		
15.		
16.		
17.		
18.		
19.		
20.		
21.		
22.		
23.		
24.		
25.		
26.		
27.		
28.		
29.		
30.		
Totals		

FUN WITH FOODS

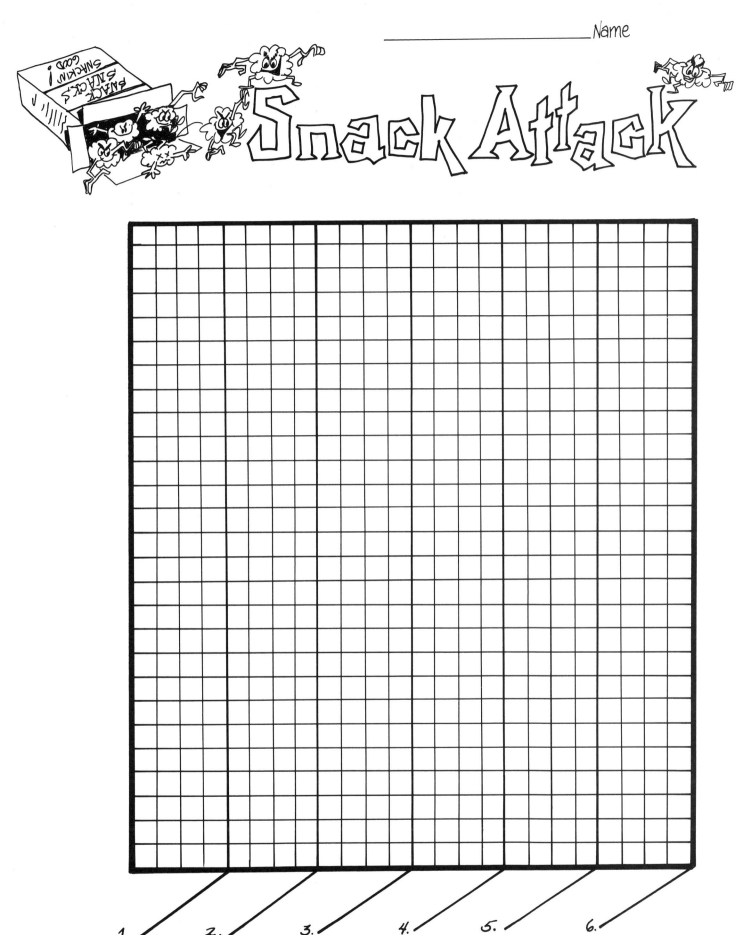

_____ Name

Snack Attack

1.   2.   3.   4.   5.   6.

_____name

Snack Attack

Circle Graph

A Seedy Experiment

I. Topic Area
Sprouts as a food source.

II. Introductory Statement
The students will discover that seeds can be sprouted easily and used as a source of fresh food.

III. Math Skills

a. Estimating
b. Subtracting
c. Averaging
d. Finding percent
e. Finding ratio

Science Processes

a. Observing
b. Measuring
c. Estimating
d. Recording data
e. Applying and generalizing
f. Controlling variables

IV. Materials

Various types of seeds* for sprouting: alfalfa, radish, mung bean, soybean, *et al.*
Paper
Metric rulers
Graduated cylinders
Paper
Metric rulers
Graduate cylinders
Scales or balances

Gram weights
Jars
Masking tape
Plastic wrap or foil
Strainers or nylon stockings

V. Key Question
"Is it possible to grow food without soil?"

VI. Background Information
The basic process for growing sprouts for food is three-fold:
1. Soak seeds in water overnight.
2. Drain, and rinse twice daily, storing in a dark cupboard until sprouts are an appropriate size for consumption.
3. Expose to light for a few hours to develop the chlorophyll.

VII. Management Suggestions
1. Have a jar for each student. Even though the process is a bit time-consuming in the initial stages, this will provide each with a project for weekend "sprout sitting."
2. For lower grades, train and use cross-age tutors from a higher grade to help the students with the first- and second-day processes.
3. Distribute the types of seeds evenly among the students so that committees can be formed for the extension activities.
4. Cut 8½ x 11 inch paper in half lengthwise for the counting of seeds.

VIII. Procedure
First Day: 30-35 minutes (can be extended over 2 days).
1. Distribute jars and seeds.
2. Fold paper lengthwise and measure a 25 cm length along the inside of the fold. Estimate how many seeds will fit along the fold. Record on student worksheet.
3. Place seeds end-to-end along fold. Count. Record on line 1.
4. Estimate weight in grams and record on line 2. Weigh and record on line 2. (For small seeds, the amount may have to be doubled.)
5. Put seeds in jar. Add 100 ml water. Estimate how much water will have been absorbed by the next day. Record on line 3.
6. Cover with foil or plastic wrap. (Put name on jar!)
7. Record observations and/or sketches on student worksheet page.

Second Day: 30 minutes.
1. Record observations. Students may wish to revise absorption estimate on line 3.
2. Drain water into another jar, using strainer or nylon stocking. Measure; subtract from 100 to find amount of water absorbed. Record on line 3.
3. Estimate and record on line 2 the weight of soaked seeds. Weigh and record on line 2.
4. Estimate number of days until sprouts will appear. Record on line 4.
5. Rinse, drain, cover lightly (leave air vent). Store in a dark area.

Third and Subsequent Days: 10-15 minutes.
1. Record observations daily.
2. Rinse and drain well twice daily.
3. When sprouts appear, estimate days to first leaf and record on line 5, and begin the measurement section on lines 6 and 7. Each day make estimates for that day only before measuring length and weight. Measurement of length can be made by placing ruler against side of jar. Those with larger seeds can weigh daily to observe growth. Smaller seeds can be weighed as soon as sprout growth is adequate for easy handling.
4. When leaves have formed, record number of days on line 5, and place in light for a few hours to "green" the leaves. Taste.
5. When a weekend intervenes, send project home for "sprout sitting," having students continue all appropriate procedures.

XI. Extension
1. Committees can be formed to compare what happened in each of the jars of each type of seeds. Comparisons can be made between different types of seeds, also.
2. Data can be averaged in a variety of categories (rate of growth, absorption, weight, etc.).
3. Data can be translated to percent or ratio, and comparisons made.
4. A study of food value of sprouts can be done (high in vitamins and minerals, low in fat).
5. Students can do more than one set of seeds simultaneously, varying the conditions and comparing/contrasting the results.
6. Have a salad day. Students can bring a variety of ingredients for salad, and include their sprouts. This could be done in conjunction with the Salad Daze experiment from this volume.
7. Students can be "teachers" for other classes.

---

* Use food grade seeds only. Those packaged for gardening have been treated with pesticides, etc.

A Seedy Experiment

Name _____

Type of Seeds _____

	Estimate	Actual
1. How many seeds are in 25 cm?	seeds	seeds
2. How much do these seeds weigh before soaking?	g	g
after soaking?	g	g
3. How much water will these seeds absorb overnight?	ml	ml
4. How long before sprouts will appear?	days	days
5. How many days after sprouting will the first leaf appear?	days	days
6. How long will an average sprout be after 1 day?	cm/mm	cm/mm
2 days?		
3 days?		
4 days?		
5 days?		
7. How much will these sprouts weigh after 1 day?	g	g
2 days?	g	g
3 days?	g	g
4 days?	g	g
5 days?	g	g

FUN WITH FOODS   20   © 1987 AIMS Education Foundation

Seedy Observations

First day : ————	Second day: ————	Third day : ————

Fourth : _____	Fifth : _____	Sixth : _____

Seventh : _____	Eighth: _____	Ninth : _____

Salad Daze

I. **Topic Area**

Improving nutrition.

II. **Introductory Statement**

By making a salad with a wide variety of ingredients, the students will try new foods and learn about nutrition.

III. **Math Skills**

a. Computing
b. Working with fractions
c. Finding ratios
d. Finding proportions
e. Finding percent
f. Graphing
g. Finding mean, mode, median, range

Science Processes

a. Observing and classifying
b. Measuring

IV. **Materials**

Wide variety of salad ingredients
Bowls, large spoon/fork
Knives
Plastic bags
Cutting board
Balance and gram weights
Graph paper

V. **Key Question**

"How can we improve the nutrition and variety of a salad?"

VI. **Background Information**

Nutritional information is available in science and health texts, at the library, and at health food stores.

VII. **Management Suggestions**

1. Having a number of balances speeds the process.
2. Base the number of ingredients on the number of committees or groups you plan.
3. If possible, wash the vegetables ahead of time.

4. Observe, examine, and weigh the vegetables in plastic bags to eliminate contamination.
5. Arrange with the cafeteria personnel to serve the salad with their lunch the day you plan this activity.

VIII. **Procedure** (to be divided into segments as your time allows)

1. Discuss properties of the various foods. Group them in different ways (type, color, size...).
2. Pass vegetables around to be held, observed, etc. (in plastic bags).
3. Rank some of them according to estimated weight.
4. Estimate weight in grams. Record on student worksheet.
5. Assign 1 vegetable to each student/group/committee. Chop, weight, record.
6. Mix salad, and eat or refrigerate, as time allows.
7. Research/discuss nutritional value of the various vegetables.
8. Graph weights of the various vegetables.
   a. Find total weight.
   b. Find difference between actual and estimated weights.
   c. Find percentage of error (difference ÷ actual).
   d. Find percentage of each ingredient of total.
   e. Express ingredients as fractions.
   f. Establish ratio for ingredients.
   g. Compute various proportions.
   h. Graph any of the above. (Make your own graph.)
   i. Sort data and teach mean, mode, median, and range.

IX. **What the Students Will Do**

1. Discuss and classify the vegetables.
2. Estimate weights.
3. Weigh the vegetables.
4. Chop ingredients.
5. Mix salad and taste new things.

X. **Discussion**

1. How did the "new" foods taste?
2. Research/discuss nutritional value of the various vegetables.

Salad Daze

Name _____

Food	WEIGHT in grams			Ratio Actual Wt. / Total Wt. Salad	Decimal	% of Total Salad
	Estimate	Actual	Difference			
1.						
2.						
3.						
4.						
5.						
6.						
7.						
8.						
9.						
10.						
11.						
12.						
13.						
14.						
15.						
16.						
17.						
18.						
19.						
20.						
21.						
TOTAL						

FRACTIONS FONDUE

I. Topic Area

A study of fractional parts and metric measurement.

II. Introductory Statement

Students will discover that they can find fractional parts everywhere, even in fondue.

III. Math Skills

a. Measuring in metric units
b. Measuring in fractional parts
c. Adding fractions
d. Writing equivalent fractions

Science Processes

a. Estimating
b. Recording data
c. Observing

IV. Materials

Balance scale with metric weights
Fondue pot (or crock pot)
Can opener
Ingredients per group of 8:
 1 large apple
 1 large pear
 1 large banana
 16 large marshmallows
 1 can chocolate syrup

Paring knives (1-3)
Cutting boards (1-3)
Toothpicks for each student
Small paper plates for each student
Paper towels

V. Key Question

"How many combinations of Fondue Fractions can you make to equal 1 whole?"

VII. Management Suggestions

1. This is a great introduction to fractions!
2. Time: Approximately 40 minutes.
3. If you are asking students to bring the ingredients, plan to begin this activity at least one day later.
4. It is best to go over the complete instructions prior to the beginning of the activity.
5. You can probably use one fondue pot for the entire class.
6. Organize the class into groups of 8 students, or use a "Panel of Experts" to demonstrate to the whole class.

VIII. Procedure

1. Have all the materials well organized.
2. Hand out the worksheets.
3. Start the fondue. Open the can of Hershey's Syrup or carob syrup and pour it into the fondue pot or crock pot. Heat it using low on the crock pot.
4. Assign groups.
5. Designate tasks: cutting, measuring, weighing, serving, etc.
6. Supervise actual investigation.

IX. What the Students Will Do

1. Estimate the total mass in grams for each ingredient. Record on worksheet.
2. Weigh ingredients separately on a metric balance and record the actual weight.
3. Cut the whole ingredients into 16 fractional parts (except marshmallows—we only use 16 marshmallows—so 1 marshmallow will be 1/16 of the total.)

 Example: Apple. Students cut the apple in half. They then cut each half into two equal parts. Cut each fourth part into 2 equal parts (fair shares). Cut each eighth into 2 equal parts. You now have 16 parts. Are they fair shares? How can you find out? Do the same for the other fruit.

4. Estimate the gram weight of one fractional piece of each ingredient and then record.
5. Weigh the estimated fractional part on a metric scale to find the actual weight. Record.
6. Divide all parts of the fruit into fair shares among the group members. Put them on paper plates.
7. Count and record the total parts of each ingredient.
8. Count and record the fair share received.
9. Write the fraction on the worksheet.
10. Complete worksheets.
11. Dip the fruit and marshmallows into the hot chocolate syrup and enjoy!

X. Discussion

1. How many combinations of Fondue Fractions can you make equal 1 whole?
2. What did you learn about fractions?
3. Can you tell something about "part versus whole"?
4. How did you divide your Fondue Fractions into fair shares?

XI. Extension

As a culmination of your unit on fractions, I suggest you do the investigation titled, "Fraction Soup."

FONDUE FRACTIONS

— Name

FRUITS	TOTAL MASS IN GRAMS		MASS OF FRACTIONAL PART in grams		HOW MANY TOTAL PARTS?	HOW MANY PARTS DID YOU GET?	WHAT IS YOUR FRACTION?
	ESTIMATE	ACTUAL	ESTIMATE	ACTUAL			
BANANA							
MARSHMALLOW							
PEAR							
APPLE							
YOUR CHOICE							
SUM							

~ RECIPE ~
serves 8

1 large apple
1 large pear
1 large banana
16 large marshmallows
1 fondue pot
1 can chocolate
(*optional: ¼ pineapple)

Estimate
Cut the fruit
Weigh
Complete the table
Dip and enjoy!

FONDUE FRACTIONS

Name _____

How many combinations of "Fondue Fractions" can you make equal to "1 whole"?

	Ex.	1.	2.	3.	4.	5.	6.	7.	8.	9.	10.	11.	12.	13.	14.	15.	16.
BANANA	$\frac{4}{16}$																
MARSHMALLOW	$\frac{4}{16}$																
PEAR	$\frac{4}{16}$																
APPLE	$\frac{4}{16}$																
SUM	$\frac{16}{16}=1$																

HEY! — Can you extend this table? If you can... continue on the back.

REMEMBER... Multiply the $\frac{\text{NUMERATOR}}{\text{DENOMINATOR}}$ BY 2,3,4,5...

WRITE 4 EQUIVALENT FRACTIONS FOR:

$\frac{1}{4} = \underline{\ \ } = \underline{\ \ } = \underline{\ \ } = \underline{\ \ }$

$\frac{1}{3} = \underline{\ \ } = \underline{\ \ } = \underline{\ \ } = \underline{\ \ }$

$\frac{1}{2} = \underline{\ \ } = \underline{\ \ } = \underline{\ \ } = \underline{\ \ }$

FUN WITH FOODS

26

© 1987 AIMS Education Foundation

FRACTION SOUP

I. Topic Area
A study of the fractional parts of vegetable soup.

II. Introductory Statement
Students will discover that they can find fractions everywhere—even in soup. They will also discover the changes that occur in food after cooking.

III. Math Skills
a. Measuring in fractions
b. Measuring in metric units
c. Graphing
d. Finding percent

Science Processes
a. Estimating
b. Recording data
c. Observing

IV. Materials
Soup Ingredients: (for group of 15)

2 carrots	1 garlic bulb (whole)
2 potatoes	6 beef bouillon cubes
1 onion	5 liters water
2 celery stalks	5 ml chili powder
1 green pepper	5 ml salt
2 tomatoes	2 ml pepper

Crock pot (or hot plate and large kettle)
1 paring knife
1 cutting board
1 colander
Student worksheets
Measuring spoons
Liter measuring set (or 1 liter empty plastic coke bottle)
Balance scale with metric weights
Large spoon for mixing
Blindfold
Student worksheets
Soup bowls (1 for each member of group or entire class)
Ladle
1 fork
Crackers for everyone
Paper towels
Cheesecloth (approximately 30 cm square)
Small piece of string
2 prizes

V. Key Question
1. "What changes occur in food during cooking?"

2. A discrepant event:
   Blindfold one-half of the students in the group. The teacher will have a sample of each of the ingredients to be used, cut into uniform pieces. The blindfolded group will be asked to smell first, then feel and taste the pieces, and identify them each time. Texture can also be discussed. The students should not be told any of the ingredients beforehand.

VII. Management Suggestions
1. This investigation can be used as a culmination of a fraction unit.
2. Timetable: The actual investigation takes from 45 minutes to 1 hour. The soup takes about 45 minutes to cook. The eating may be done in about 30 minutes. (You can do another activity while the soup is cooking.)
3. If students have never worked with metric weights, it's a good idea to let them have hands-on experience before the investigation. Use numerous small objects found in the classroom and let everyone estimate the gram weight and then actually weigh the object.
4. Fraction Soup takes less time to complete if you spend time beforehand acquainting the students with just exactly what they are going to do.
5. Have the students bring in the vegetables and materials 2 days before the investigation. What they have forgotten, you can bring.
6. Small groups of 5-10 work best if you have good adult supervision. If not, you can use a "Panel of Experts" (one group) to demonstrate to the entire class. You would still have all students estimating, but just one group doing all the cutting and weighing.
7. The ingredients listed serve 15 people. Double the recipe to feed an entire class.

VIII. Procedure
1. Have all the materials well organized. Hand out student worksheets.
2. Do the discrepant event (see Key Question). Cut 2-3 small uniform cubes of each vegetable for this.
3. Assign groups.
4. Designate tasks: cutting, measuring, weighing, cooking, etc.
5. Supervise actual investigation.

IX. What the Students Will Do

1. Estimate the total mass in grams for each type of vegetable. Students then will record their estimate on worksheet.

2. Weigh the vegetables separately on a metric balance and then record the actual total weight.

3. Cut the whole vegetable into fractional parts according to the recipe. (Example: Potato. Cut the potato in half. Just to check whether or not you have divided the potato into fair shares, put one half on each side of the scale to see how equally you cut them. Then cut each potato half into two equal parts (fair shares). Cut each fourth into two equal parts. Cut each eighth into two equal parts. Your potato is now cut into sixteenths. The recipe called for 2 potatoes so you have 32 total potato parts or 32 fair shares.

4. At this time, set aside the whole, unpeeled garlic bulb to be placed in the pot later.

5. Estimate the mass of one fractional part of each vegetable and then record the estimate on student worksheet.

6. Weigh each estimated vegetable part separately and then record the actual weight before cooking.

7. Count the total parts of each vegetable and record.

8. Set aside each weighed fractional part. These "fractions" are to be placed in cheesecloth and tied firmly with a piece of string. These "fractions" will be weighed after cooking. (Include 1 bouillon cube in your cheesecloth.)

9. Wash all the vegetable parts and drain in a colander.

10. Put the vegetables, including the whole unpeeled garlic, into a big pot. Measure 5 liters of water into the pot. Then add the remaining ingredients and the cheesecloth bundle.

11. Cook (bring to a boil and cook on medium) at least 30 minutes or until fork enters the pototo easily. Do not overcook!

12. Remove the cheesecloth and allow the cooked vegetables inside to cool.

13. Estimate the weight of each "fraction" of vegetables after cooking and record.

14. Before eating, each student counts how many parts of each vegetable they find in their soup. Record on student worksheet.

15. Serve the Fraction Soup! Pass out the crackers and enjoy!

16. Find the Mystery Fraction! When serving the soup, tell students that one bowl of soup will have a mystery fraction which they will not eat. The student with a whole garlic bulb in his soup will get a prize. Each student will estimate how many cloves of garlic are in the whole garlic bulb. Have all the students write down their estimate of this mystery fraction on worksheet, page 18. The mystery-bowl student will then count the cloves. The student closest to the estimate also receives a prize.

17. When finished, weigh the cooled vegetable "fractions" that were cooked in the cheesecloth.

18. Record the mass of each fractional part after cooking.

19. Complete all worksheets.

X. Discussion

1. What changes occur in food during cooking? (Food changes consistency, loses water.)

2. What other things beside "soup" might contain fractions? (Fruit...)

3. Were your estimates close to actual weights?

4. Was there a change in the weight of the vegetables after cooking? Why? (Heat and water absorption and evaporation.)

5. What happened to the water level in the soup pot? Explain. (Level went down due to evaporation.)

6. When the lid is taken off the soup pot, what is on the inside of the lid? Explain. (Water, not soup, because of evaporation.)

7. Why is "Fraction Soup" good for you? (Nutrients.)

XI. Extension

1. Do the Enrichment Activity on student worksheet.

2. Make a comparison graph for nutrients.

3. Make a tally of what food groups we have and what we need to make complete food group in Fraction Soup.

4. Do investigation entitled "Fondue Fractions."

FRACTION SOUP

NAME _____

RECIPE

2 carrots cut into sixteenths
2 celery stalks cut into eighths
2 potatoes cut into sixteenths
1 onion cut into fourths
1 green pepper cut into eighths
2 tomatoes cut into halves
1 whole garlic bulb - do not peel - leave whole
6 beef bouillon cubes
5 litres water
5 ml chili powder
5 ml salt
2 ml pepper

(this recipe serves 15)

VEGETABLES	TOTAL MASS IN GRAMS		MASS OF 1 FRACTIONAL PART (BEFORE COOKING)		MASS OF 1 FRACTIONAL PART (AFTER COOKING)		TOTAL PARTS
	ESTIMATE	ACTUAL	ESTIMATE	ACTUAL	ESTIMATE	ACTUAL	
2 Carrots							
2 stalks celery							
2 Potatoes							
1 Peeled onion							
1 Green Pepper without stem							
2 tomatoes							
TOTAL							

FRACTION SOUP

MY RECORD

COUNT THE PIECES	Total PARTS	PARTS in MY BOWL	MY FRACTION
CARROTS			
CELERY			
POTATOES			
ONIONS			
GREEN PEPPER			
TOMATOES			
TOTAL			

How many cloves of garlic do you think are in an entire garlic bulb?

MY ESTIMATE OF THE

MYSTERY FRACTION?

PERCENTAGE PAGE

Find the percentage of each of the soup ingredients used.

INGREDIENT	VEGETABLE WEIGHT	RATIO TOTAL WEIGHT	RATIO VEGETABLE WEIGHT / SOUP'S TOTAL WEIGHT	DECIMAL	PERCENTAGE %
2 carrots					
2 stalks celery					
2 potatoes					
1 onion					
1 Green pepper					
2 tomatoes					
1 garlic					
6 bouillon cubes					
5 litres water					
5 ml chili powder					
5 ml salt					
2 ml pepper					

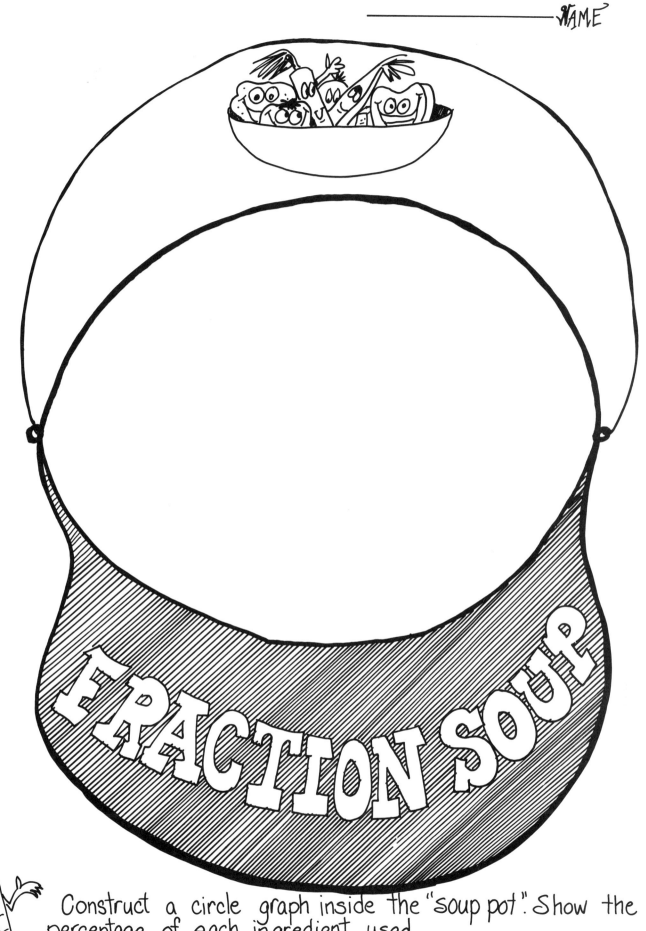

Construct a circle graph inside the "soup pot". Show the percentage of each ingredient used.

Better Butter

I. Topic Area
Changes in appearance, and measurement of volume.

II. Introductory Statement
Very often the source of common foods is unknown. Butter is a food which is contained within a liquid. The students will enjoy separating the butter from the cream and sampling their product.

III. Math Skills
a. Subtracting
b. Finding percent
c. Graphing
d. Measuring solids and liquids

Science Processes
a. Observing
b. Recording data
c. Comparing data
d. Generalizing

IV. Materials
Baby food jars with lids
2 pints each of 2 brands of whipping cream
Large bowl of cold water
Fine mesh strainer
Masking tape
Marking pens
Metric measuring cups
Balance scale and weights *or* diet scale
Small plastic bowls for use with diet scale
Bowls for butter storage
Student worksheets

V. Key Question
"Is the ratio of butter to cream the same for all brands of cream?"

VI. Background Information
Butterfat can be separated from light whipping cream or heavy cream. Light cream contains 30% to 40% fat and heavy cream contains no less than 36%.

The cream can be separated into butter and buttermilk. This can be done by shaking the cream in a tightly closed jar or beating it in a bowl with an electric mixer. Shaking incorporates air and causes the cream to increase its volume. Continue to shake the cream and it will suddenly turn to liquid again, as it separates, yielding butter and buttermilk. The fat globules will adhere to each other and form a soft yellow mass known as butter. The buttermilk is thin, not at all like cultured buttermilk.

VII. Management Suggestions
1. Divide the class into 4 groups.
2. Prepare the labeled jars before class begins.
3. Establish a "weigh station" for weighing the products before and after.
4. Older cream turns to butter faster.

VIII. Procedure
1. Bring the cream to room temperature and label all jars.
2. Prepare a large bowl with cold water to rinse the butter.
3. Set up scales.
4. Prepare chalkboard or overhead model. Write the name and price of each brand of cream on the chalkboard.
5. As a demonstration, put 1 tablespoon of cream into a baby food jar. Tighten the lid and shake the jar until separation occurs. Pour the buttermilk out into a container. Demonstrate the rinsing process (put butter into strainer and "swish" in water in bowl). Explain that what remains is butter and that it will be measured to find out what percent of the cream was butter.
6. The students then weigh their samples and take turns shaking the jars. Remind them to pour off the buttermilk as soon as the butter forms.

IX. What the Students Will Do
1. Weigh, shake, drain, rinse and reweigh samples.
2. Subtract to find the weight of the buttermilk. Record. Compute the percentage.
3. Graph the results.

X. Discussion
1. Did all the samples contain the same amount of butter?
2. Are the 100 and 220 gram samples equal?
3. How does brand A compare to brand B?
4. How do you account for the results?

XI. Extension
1. Compute the cost of homemade butter and compare it to a pound of prepackaged butter. Percentages from your experiment can be used.
2. Conduct a taste survey comparing home brand A, brand B, and margarine.
3. Use your butter with the "Popcorn Comparison" investigation.
4. Make cottage cheese and compare percentages of cheese and whey.

_____ Name

Better Butter

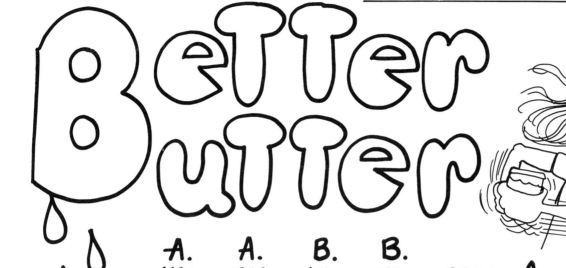

A.	A.	B.	B.
100g	200g	100g	200g

RATIO

BUTTER
_____

CREAM

PERCENT %

90
80
70
60
50
40
30
20
10
0

1. 2.   1. 2.   1. 2.   1. 2.

1. CREAM   2. BUTTERMILK

GRAPH THE % OF BUTTER

BRAND **A** : _____ ml

NAME _____

PRICE _____

BRAND **B** : _____ ml

NAME _____

PRICE _____

A. $\dfrac{}{\text{(A) } 100} = \dfrac{}{\text{(A) } 200}$

$\dfrac{}{\text{(A) } 100} = \dfrac{}{\text{(B) } 100}$

FILL IN THE
% OF BUTTER
IN EACH RATIO
THEN MARK
THE EQUAL SIGNS
AS
$=$ or $\neq$

B. $\dfrac{}{\text{(B) } 100} = \dfrac{}{\text{(B) } 200}$

$\dfrac{}{\text{(A) } 200} = \dfrac{}{\text{(B) } 200}$

CONCLUSION: _____

_____

_____

_____

© 1987 AIMS Education Foundation

Better Butter

_____ Name

BRAND **A.** _____ ml

NAME _____
PRICE _____

BRAND **B.** _____ ml

NAME _____
PRICE _____

BUTTER + BUTTERMILK = CREAM

A. _____ g + _____ g = 100 g CREAM _____ % BUTTER

A. _____ g + _____ g = 200 g CREAM _____ % BUTTER

B. _____ g + _____ g = 100 g CREAM _____ % BUTTER

B. _____ g + _____ g = 200 g CREAM _____ % BUTTER

How much butter would you get from a whole carton of cream?

_____

What is the cost of the butter?

_____

WHICH TASTES BETTER... BRAND A OR BRAND B?

35

MY-O-MAYO

I. Topic Area

The making of an emulsion, specifically mayonnaise.

II. Introductory Statement

Students will discover that mayonnaise is an emulsion of oil and water with the emulsifying agent being egg or egg yolks.

III. Math Skills / Science Processes

Math Skills
a. Measuring volume
b. Computing whole numbers and decimals
c. Subtracting of decimals
d. Finding percent
e. Using a formula

Science Processes
a. Observing
b. Controlling variables
c. Recording data
d. Interpreting data
e. Predicting

IV. Materials

Pint jar with lid
Blender or electric mixer
Mixing bowl (small)
Measuring spoons (metric or standard)
Spatula
2 empty quart jars with lids
Paper towels
ml measuring cups (or standard)
1-2 eggs
Salt
Dry mustard
Vegetable oil
Vinegar
Lemon juice

V. Key Question

"Is there anything we can do to keep oil and water from separating?"

VI. Background Information

An emulsion is a preparation of an oily substance (vegetable oil) held in suspension in a watery liquid (vinegar or lemon juice) by means of an emulsifier. An emulsifier is a substance such as gelatin, gum, arabic, or egg yolk for emulsifying a fixed oil.

Begin by explaining that when oil and vinegar separate, the oil droplets grow larger and larger until they come together to form a separate layer. The addition of certain third substances to such a mixture of oil and water prevents the oil droplets from coming together so that there is no separation into layers. The result is a stable mixture of two liquids called an emulsion. The substance that keeps the oil droplets apart is called the emulsifying agent. Mayonnaise is an emulsion of oil in water (vinegar or lemon juice) and the emulsifying agent is the egg or egg yolk.

The idea in making mayonnaise is to spread tiny droplets of oil evenly through the egg or egg yolks. The egg yolk coats these droplets as they form and prevents them from coming together and forming a separate layer of oil. For this reason, the oil must be added slowly. Your students will be able to tell when the emulsion has formed because the mixture will thicken. Once this happens they can add oil slightly faster until the full cup has been beaten into the yolks.

VII. Management Suggestions

1. This should be done either as a small group activity (3-5 students) or as a whole-class investigation by having a panel of experts demonstrate for the class.
2. A glass bowl is best for the mixer method as they can see the emulsion forming.
3. It is best to talk about why the oil and water separate before you begin the investigation (i.e., droplets of oil become larger).

VIII. Procedure

1. As a demonstration, put a mixture of oil and water in the pint jar, shake vigorously and have students observe as mixture separates.
2. Begin investigation by measuring egg or egg yolk, salt, dry mustard, and vinegar or lemon juice into blender container or mixing bowl. (All ingredients must be room temperature.) See student worksheet for recipe.
3. If using blender, mix for 70 seconds adding oil in a steady stream through opening in top while motor is running.
4. If using electric hand mixer, beat at medium speed until the egg yolks are sticky. Add the oil by teaspoonfuls until mixture thickens, then add oil slightly faster until all has been beaten into the egg yolks.
5. Using rubber spatula, scrape into ml container to measure the volume.
6. Put into empty jars and refrigerate until used (will keep several weeks).

IX. What the Students Will Do

1. As ingredients are measured, record on chart and add to find total volume of the ingredients.
2. Before beating in the oil, students should predict whether the volume will increase or decrease. (It usually decreases.)
3. After mayonnaise is made, measure volume and record on chart. Compute the difference, then using formula compute the percent of change.

X. Discussion

1. Did the volume increase or decrease? Why?
2. Did all the mixtures thicken? Why or why not?
3. Why didn't the oil and water separate? After discussion, explain about emulsions (see Background Information).
4. Can we change the method of preparation or the order in which we add the ingredients and still make mayonnaise?

XI. Extension

1. Try variations such as adding all the ingredients at once to see if it will still form an emulsion.
2. Students may want to weigh the ingredients and compute changes in weight in grams.
3. Use your mayonnaise to make salad dressing, the "Perfect Sandwich", a dip or potato salad.
4. A cost analysis can be done comparing homemade or purchased mayonnaise.
5. Mayonnaise Cake is an easy, moist, non-frosted cake that all ages enjoy. It could be served with the ice cream from the "I Scream" investigation.
6. Advanced students might want to investigate other types of emulsions and how they are formed.

RECIPE – MAYONNAISE CAKE

1 cup chopped dates	2 cups flour
1 tsp. baking soda	½ tsp. salt
1 tsp. vanilla	1 tbsp. cocoa
1 cup sugar	1 cup mayonnaise
1 cup boiling water	1 cup chopped nuts

Put dates, soda, vanilla, and sugar in a large mixing bowl. Pour the boiling water over and let set until lukewarm. While it is cooling, combine flour, salt, and cocoa in a small mixing bowl.

Add dry mixture to the first and mix well. Then stir in the mayonnaise and nuts.

Put in a 9x13 greased and floured pan and bake for 45 minutes at 325°

_____Name

MY-O-MAYO

Blender Recipe

1 egg
15 ml (1 TBSP) lemon juice
2.5 ml (½ tsp.) salt
1.25 ml (¼ tsp.) dry mustard
240 ml (1 cup) vegetable oil

Put first 4 ingredients in the blender. Mix 70 seconds adding oil in a steady stream.

Mixer Recipe

2 egg yolks
30 ml (2 TBSP) Vinegar
2.5 ml (½ tsp.) salt
1.25 ml (¼ tsp.) dry mustard
240 ml (1 cup) vegetable oil

Put first 4 ingredients in bowl. Mix at medium speed adding oil a few drops at a time until thick. Then add remaining oil faster. (TAKES 5-7 minutes)

My Prediction : The volume will   a. increase ☐   b. decrease ☐   check one!

Ingredients	VOLUME Blender	Mixer
EGG	ml	ml
SALT	ml	ml
MUSTARD	ml	ml
VINEGAR OR LEMON JUICE	ml	ml
VEGETABLE OIL	ml	ml
TOTAL	ml	ml

	VOLUME Blender	Mixer
TOTAL OF INGREDIENTS	ml	ml
MAYONAISE	ml	ml
AMOUNT OF CHANGE	ml	ml
PERCENT OF CHANGE	%	%

The volume   a. increased ☐   b. decreased ☐   CHECK ONE!

To FIND THE PERCENT OF CHANGE TAKE:

$$\frac{\text{AMOUNT OF CHANGE}}{\text{TOTAL VOLUME OF INGREDIENTS}} \times 100 = \% \text{ OF CHANGE}$$

I. Topic Area

A study of the change of liquid to a semi-solid state due to a change in temperature.

II. Introduction

The students will discover that as the ice melts, the ice cream mixture solidifies.

III. Math Skills

a. Computing ratio
b. Measuring
c. Problem solving

Science Processes

a. Observing
b. Measuring
c. Recording data

IV. Materials

Ingredients per recipe for ice cream
Graduated cylinder (measuring cup)
Gram scale and masses
Mixing bowl—glass, if available
Measuring spoons, metric/standard
Rubber spatula
Mixer, hand or electric
Rock salt, 4.5 kg (10 lbs.) (About 300 gm (11 oz) of salt and ice for 1 "freezer" of 1:1 ratio)
Crushed ice—3.4 kg (7½ lb)

—*For each "freezer":*

1 tongue depressor
1 170 ml (6 oz) juice can (thoroughly washed). Note: frozen juice cans are paper. Use tomato or fruit juice cans from the juice shelves in the grocery.
1 bottom half of a half-gallon milk carton cut 2 cm shorter than the juice can (about 8 cm from bottom of carton)

Recipe for ice cream: Mix together and beat well.

INGREDIENTS	SERVES:			
	28	21	14	7
Eggs	4	3	2	1
Sugar	480 ml (16 oz)	360 ml (12 oz)	240 ml (8 oz)	120 ml (4 oz)
Half & half ...	2400 ml (80 oz)	1800 ml (60 oz)	1200 ml (40 oz)	600 ml (20 oz)
Vanilla	20 ml 3/4 t.	15 ml 1/2 t.	10 ml 1/4 t.	5 ml 1/8 t.

V. Key Question

"How much salt does an ice-water mixture need to freeze ice cream most efficiently?"

VI. Background Information

Freezing ice cream depends on cold water and not on the ice itself. When ice melts, it absorbs heat, which makes its temperature rise. Since salt causes ice to melt faster, more heat is absorbed, this time from the ice cream mixture. Stirring adds air and keeps it smooth. Too much salt freezes it too fast, which decreases quality. Too little ice, and... Since the purpose of this investigation is to determine the optimum ratio of salt to ice, we want the fastest freeze with the best quality.

VII. Management Suggestions

1. Mix enough of the ingredients ahead of time to serve 7.
2. Prepare 7 different "freezers" with 7 different ratios of salt to ice masses: 100% ice, 1:10, 1:8, 1:5, 1:4, 1:2, 1:1. The salt and ice needs to be mixed together, perhaps in 6 different half gallon milk cartons, so that more of the mixture can be added as the ice melts.
3. The class can be divided into 7 groups or it can be done as a demonstration by a "panel of experts."
4. Note the time of beginning and check at intervals to examine consistency and quality. Continue stirring until frozen or you give up. This should freeze in 10 to 15 minutes.
5. Make a freezer or 2 (1 gallon) of ice cream using the information about the best ratio to maximize the efficiency so everyone can have some to eat, or make enough individual "freezers" for every student to make his own.
6. Time required: about 45 minutes.

IX. What the Students Will Do

1. Weigh the crushed ice and salt to make the ratio of salt to ice that they will use. Each "freezer" will require 100 g of ice.
2. Fill the juice can half full with the ice cream mixture.
3. Place juice can in center of milk carton and fill carton to top with ice/salt mixture.
4. Stir with tongue depressor until mixture freezes. Add more ice/salt mixture as needed.
5. When some of the ice creams are frozen, determine if there is a difference in the quality, and if so, which is best.

X. Discussion

1. What is the main ingredient in determining the time it takes to freeze ice cream?
2. What caused the ice cream to freeze?
3. Could you notice a difference in the texture?
4. Which seems to be the best ratio?

XI. Extension

1. Try again, but this time add water before beginning to stir to see if this first melting process speeds up the freezing process. Be sure to have a place for the overflow.
2. Do again, this time using thermometers to plot the drop of temperature for each ice/salt ratio. The use of a metal "gourmet" thermometer, while expensive, may be cheaper than broken glass thermometers. Prepare for a temperature of −17 °C (0 °F) or colder.
3. Add fresh fruit for new flavor.

Burns, Marilyn. *Good For Me!* Boston: Little, Brown and Co., 1978.

Wilms, Barbara. *Crunchy Bananas*, Santa Barbara: Sagamore Books, 1975.

I SCREAM!

HOW DOES SALT AFFECT
THE FREEZING OF ICE CREAM?
RECORD THE TEMPERATUTURES OF
THE DIFFERENT RATIOS EVERY 5 MINUTES, AND DESCRIBE THE CONSISTENCY.

Consistency Description After:

SALT : ICE RATIO	5 min.	10 min.	15 min.	20 min.	25 min.	30 min.
100% ICE						
1 : 10						
1 : 8						
1 : 5						
1 : 4						
1 : 2						
1 : 1						

CONTINUE STIRRING
UNTIL FROZEN →

FREEZER →

CUT 2cm SHORTER THAN
JUICE CAN

MILK
½ GAL.

WASH
WELL

JUICE
CAN
6oz.

ICE
700g

TONGUE DEPRESSOR

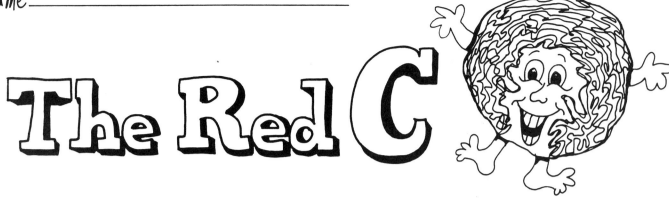

The Red C

I. Topic Area
Chemistry: acids and bases

II. Introductory Statement
Students will use red cabbage juice as an acid-base indicator to test a variety of liquids.

III. Math Skills
a. Using numeration
b. Problem solving
c. Measuring by drops

Science Processes
a. Observing
b. Predicting
c. Recording data
d. Interpreting data

IV. Materials
For the red cabbage juice:
  1 medium-sized red cabbage
  saucepan
  boiling water
  cup or pitcher for pouring cabbage juice
For each group: 1 oz. of each solution:
  lemon juice
  milk
  baking soda and water mixture
  liquid detergent
  apple juice
  uncolored carbonated drink
  sea or salt water
  washing soda and water mixture
  tomato juice
  tap water
  ammonia
  milk of magnesia
  optional: other solutions
     *   *   *   *   *
  1 oz. plastic cup for each solution
  pipet or eye dropper for cabbage juice
  4 oz. cup for cabbage juice
  stir stick for each solution tested
  white paper

V. Key Question
"If you tasted some lemon juice without sugar in it, how would it taste?"

VI. Background Information
The water solutions of acids contain hydrogen. When acids are dissolved in water, the water molecules and the hydrogen molecules

together form charged particles called hydronium ions. Stronger acids produce more hydronium ions; weaker acids produce fewer hydronium ions. There is citric acid in lemon, orange, and grapefruit juices. There is carbonic acid and phosphoric acid in carbonated drinks. These can be tasted safely and have a sour taste. Stronger acids such as those used for automobile batteries are very dangerous and can be harmful if not used properly. They can burn the skin and make holes in clothing.

Bases contain hydrogen and oxygen; most have at least one metal in them. When dissolved in water they produce hydroxide ions. The major ingredient of milk of magnesia is magnesium hydroxide. Bases may feel slippery and taste bitter. Their water solutions react with acids to form salts. Bases are useful for cleaning because they break down grease.

An acid-base indicator is a dye used to distinguish between acidic and basic solutions by means of color changes. There are many different acid-base indicators in use in chemistry laboratories. A good example of a commonly used acid-base indicator is a test kit for swimming pool water. In this lesson, red cabbage juice is used as an acid-base indicator. Acid solutions will turn pink or a deeper red, while basic (alkaline) solutions will turn green (weak) or yellow (strong).

VII. Management
1. Beforehand or at the beginning of the activity, make the red cabbage juice. (Note: Red cabbage leaves may be obtained at no cost by requesting trimmings at a supermarket.) Cut half the cabbage into chunks, place in saucepan, and cover with boiling water. (You can also use a food processor; the smaller the pieces, the less water needed, and the stronger the juice.) Boil until cabbage loses its color or at least five minutes. Cool and refrigerate until use. It should be a purplish-blue.
2. Beforehand, number or label small cups for solutions to be tested. (The advantage of the smaller cups is that very little of each solution is required. With younger students you may wish to substitute larger containers such as baby food jars, so that students can handle them more easily. Use only clear containers so students can see the color changes.)
3. Have students place all containers on white paper so that color changes may be seen easily.

VIII. Procedure
1. Discuss the *Key Question:* "If you tasted some lemon juice without sugar in it, how would it taste?" Explain that a sour taste means a liquid is an acid and that some solutions are acids while others are bases.
CAUTION: Warn students that although we know that

some substances are acid because they taste sour, we should not smell or taste unknown substances without adult supervision, because some are very dangerous.

2. Divide students into groups. Explain that some liquids are acids while others are bases; we are going to test several liquids using red cabbage juice. Distribute activity sheets and have them list liquids which they will test. (We suggest testing lemon juice first since the class has just discussed its sour taste.) If cabbage juice was made beforehand, pass some raw cabbage around the class for students to observe.

3. Place white paper under cups so color changes can be observed easily. Fill 4-ounce cups with cabbage juice. Distribute pipets. If necessary, practice filling and then squeezing out single drops.

4. Half-fill a 1-ounce cup with the first liquid you have listed. Have students predict whether it is an acid or a base by checking the appropriate box. Use pipets to add cabbage juice drop-by-drop until there is a color change. Caution them not to add too much, to stir after each addition, and not to use the pipet for anything but cabbage juice.

5. Note any color change. Pink or red will indicate an acid, green or yellow a base. Record test results on the activity sheet. (If your students can control a pipet well, you may wish to let them put a drop of the actual solution in the appropriate square on the activity sheet. Be sure not to use the same pipet as used for the cabbage juice.)

6. Repeat the prediction and test on each solution.

IX. Discussion

1. What does red cabbage juice do?
2. Which solutions are acids? Are some stronger acids than others? [remind them that more water will usually produce a weaker solution]
3. How did testing your first solution help you with your predictions?
4. Why do we want to know the difference between an acid and a base? [They have different effects on other substances:
- A strong acid would burn your skin
- Acids and bases would tend to neutralize each other. (Neutralize means to weaken an acid or a base and bring the two closer in pH to one another.)]
5. Balancing the pH is very important in a swimming pool. What happens if the acids and bases are not properly balanced? [skin dries, eyes burn, bacteria grow, algae grows]

X. Extensions

1. Discuss the terms *acid* and *base* in more detail. Predict and test other substances such as shampoo, distilled vinegar, cream of tartar (hydrogen tartrate), sour milk (curds removed).
2. Make turmeric paper
   You will need: zip-type plastic bag
                    2 ml turmeric powder (spice)
                    100 ml alcohol
                    coffee filters
                    cookie sheet or plastic
                    quart bowl
   In a quart bowl, stir turmeric into the alcohol. Dip one coffee filter at a time into this solution. Place wet filters on the cookie

sheet to dry. (Since turmeric will stain, wipe up any spills immediately and do not place on paper towels.) Cut the dry papers into strips about one-half inch by three inches. Store the strips in the plastic bag. The resulting dry turmeric paper is a bright yellow, and will turn red in strong bases such as ammonia.

3. Challenge students to research and test other pH indicators such as grape juice or fuschia berries.

4. If you add cabbage juice to soda water, heat, and then retest, you will have a much stronger alkaline or base. You will have produced sodium carbonate from sodium bicarbonate!

5. Have students watch the news for accounts of chemical spills. See if the report tells what was spilled and if something was used to neutralize it. What should be used if ammonia (a strong base which can be a poisonous gas) is spilled? [an acid, such as vinegar]

XI. Curriculum Correlations

Language arts: Read labels from containers of lye, ammonia, etc., noting especially the directions for neutralizing them in case of external contact or internal consumption. Milk of magnesia would have comments about its antacid properties. Many shampoos are advertised as "pH-balanced."

Name —————————

The Red C

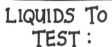

Substance	CABBAGE WATER			
	ESTIMATE		ACTUAL	
	ACID (pink)	BASE (green)	ACID (pink)	BASE (green)

LIQUIDS TO TEST:

lemon juice
milk
baking soda water
liquid detergent
apple juice
uncolored carbonated drink
sea or salt water
washing soda water
tomato juice
tap water
ammonia

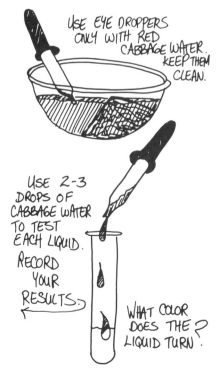

USE EYE DROPPERS ONLY WITH RED CABBAGE WATER. KEEP THEM CLEAN.

USE 2-3 DROPS OF CABBAGE WATER TO TEST EACH LIQUID.

RECORD YOUR RESULTS.

WHAT COLOR DOES THE LIQUID TURN?

How Sweet It Is...

I. Topic Area
Chemical change.

II. Introductory Statement
Students will become aware that most common foods contain simple sugars, and be able to rank the foods tested according to the amount of sugar contained.

III. Math Skills
a. Ranking from least to greatest

Science Processes
a. Chemical change
b. Interpreting data

IV. Materials
The liquid form of each food to be tested
Test tubes—minimum of two for each food that will be tested
Graduated cylinder, by milliliters
Eye dropper
"Clinitest" tablets and color chart—"2 drop method"
Blender
Funnel
Filter paper
Clock or watch with a second hand
Test tube rack
Two containers for water
Student worksheet

V. Key Question
"Which has more sugar, an onion or a lemon?"

VI. Background Information
1. "Clinitest" tablets are made of caustic soda and can burn the skin if handled with bare hands. Pour one tablet into the lid of the bottle and then drop tablet into test tube. Recap immediately.
2. Care should be taken to keep tablets from collecting moisture. Do not allow water to get into the bottle of tablets.
3. The chemical reaction of "Clinitest" tablets in the liquid creates heat. Hold test tube at the top of the tube only. For added safety use test tube holder.
4. If the result of this reaction is at the maximum limit, repeat, diluting the solution each time until the color falls within the limits of the chart.
5. Since most test tube racks hold 6 tubes, that would seem to be the number of food samples to try at one time. If you test more foods, use 2 sheets side by side.
6. To arrive at the 1½ drops solution, use 3 drops solution and 3 drops water to form a dilute solution. Then use three drops of this diluted solution and nine drops of water to make the 1½:10½ mixture.

VII. Management Suggestions
1. Select 4-6 students to be a "panel of experts." They can prepare the solutions for the class to use in small groups, or they can do the investigation as a demonstration.

2. Entire activity could be done in two 45-minute periods, or one new food with each different period, recording and sharing the results with the following classes.
3. After having students rank the foods being tested, use a drop of the dilute solution on the tongue to see if they would change their ranking. Have students hold their noses while doing this. This will require more concentrate. Or have half the class rank visually while the other half ranks by taste.

VIII. Procedure
1. In a blender, finely chop any solid food (apple, potato, carrot, onion, etc.) that you wish to test.
2. Add 10 ml of water to a graduated cylinder.
3. Dampen a sheet of filter paper; put filter and funnel directly into graduated cylinder. Squeeze the chopped food to extract the liquid into the funnel until the level of the solution reaches 12 ml. Rinse equipment after each use.
4. Pour into a test tube for future use. If using juice of orange, lime, grapefruit, etc., the process is a lot neater.
5. Shake the test tube of solution to get an even concentrate, then drop 12 drops of this solution into another test tube. Add a "Clinitest" tablet and record the results on the student sheet. Rinse dropper after each use.
6. If the result is at the limit of the chart, repeat step 5 using 6 drops of each solution and water. Repeat step 5 (see test 3 and 4 on student sheet) until the result falls within the range of the chart.
7. If tests 2, 3, or 4 were needed, multiply the indicated percent by the test number to arrive at the percent level of sugar in that food.
8. At this point have the students rank the foods being tested from least to greatest including the lemon and onion in their proper ranking.

IX. What the Students Will Do
1. Answer the key question.
2. Observe and record data for each test done.
3. Estimate the ranking of the foods tested.
4. Rank results and compare with estimates.

X. Discussion
1. Did the amount of sugar in some foods appear to be more or less than you expected?
2. Why did some foods appear to have no sugar?
3. Is the result of our test the total amount of sugars in the food?
4. Do some foods require chemicals to change other (starch) elements to sugar?

XI. Extension
1. Test for acidity/alkalinity.
2. Test for starch.
3. Determine calorie content from sugar content.
4. Estimate amount of sugar in your daily diet.

How Sweet It Is...

"Which has more sugar, an onion or a lemon?"

Rank (by estimate) the sugar content of the 6 foods being tested in order from least to greatest. Then estimate the percent of sugar content in each food.

____ < ____ < ____ < ____ < ____ < ____

____ %   ____ %   ____ %   ____ %   ____ %   ____ %

Now, do the test:

Food	Lemon											
TEST 1												
TEST 2												
TEST 3												
TEST 4												
	COLOR	%	COLOR	%	COLOR	%	COLOR	%	COLOR	%	COLOR	%

Now that you know, rank the 6 foods again and compare with your estimate.

____ < ____ < ____ < ____ < ____ < ____

____ %   ____ %   ____ %   ____ %   ____ %   ____ %

TEST 1 = 12 drops solution, 0 drops H_2O
TEST 2 = 6 drops solution, 6 drops H_2O
TEST 3 = 3 drops solution, 9 drops H_2O
TEST 4 = 1½ drops solution, 10½ drops H_2O

PAPER CAPER

I. Topic Area
Absorption rate of paper towels.

II. Introductory Statement
Students will become aware of the cost/absorption efficiency of paper towels.

III. Math Skills   Science Processes
a. Averaging   a. Observing
b. Graphing
c. Establishing proportions
d. Using formulas
e. Measuring

IV. Materials
One or more ring stands or camera tripods with center post
Scissors
1 sheet each of various brands of paper towels
Metric ruler
Water soluble marking pen
2 or 3 clear plastic or glass containers
Stop watch
Student worksheets

V. Key Question
"Are all paper towels created equal?"

VI. Background Information
The water will "travel" up the paper towel against the gravitational pull by capillary action or attraction.

The grain of the paper can be determined by tearing a paper towel from top to bottom and from side to side. If it tears straight from edge to edge that will be "with the grain".

If a micrometer is available, towel thickness can be measured to be used as a comparison. All decimal answers are rounded to hundredths.

To change from square feet to square meters, use the ratio of 1:.0929 (1 square foot = .929 square meters). To find the price per square meter, divide the price by the number of square meters.

To find the cost efficiency, divide "average of trials" by "price per m²". (Round the answer to tenths.)

VII. Management Suggestions
A "panel of experts" of 2 or 3 pairs of students can prepare the materials before the investigation takes place. On one sheet of each brand of paper towel have the students mark 5 cm wide strips the length of the paper and going with the grain of the paper. Mark two lines parallel to the end grain edge; one .5 cm from the edge in ball point pen, the other 5 cm from the same edge in a fine line water soluble marking pen. (Suggestion: use a red "Pilot Precise Ball Liner.") Cut three strips of each brand of paper towel, staple them together with a label of the brand, number of plys and thickness for future use with the class. Depending on the number of towels to be tested, this investigation can be done in about two to three 45-minute periods.

VIII. Procedure
1. *Ask:* How many seconds will it take the water to reach the line? *Do:* Dip .5 cm of a 5 cm wide strip of marked paper towel into a clear container with about 1 cm of water. Watch and note the time until the line begins to bleed from the water that has reached the line through capillary attraction. (This may be expanded to any number of brands of paper towel you wish to use to introduce into this investigation.

2. With the panel working in pairs, one to lower the towel into the water to the .5 cm line, the other to observe the time, have them test each brand of towel three times. (Time needed for each strip will vary from about ½ minute to 4 minutes, depending on the brand.)

IX. What the Students Will Do

1. The panel of expert students will scotch tape the towel to the ring so that it does not shift position.
2. One of the students will lower the ring so that the paper towel dips into the water to the .5 cm line.
3. The second student starts the watch when the towel touches the water and stops it when the ink begins to bleed.
4. The class observes and records on the table of information the times as given after all three trials of each brand are tested.
5. They then find the average time, the price per square meter, and the cost efficiency. It may also be necessary to convert from square feet to square meters.
6. On the "rate of absorption graph" write the name of each brand to be tested. This should be standardized with all 1-ply towels named before all 2-ply towels, etc.
7. Then graph the average time of the three trials for each brand.
8. On the "price comparison graph" graph the name of the least expensive to most expensive towel as determined on the "price per m²" column on the table of information.
9. Use the distance formula, d = rt, to determine how long, at this rate, it would take the water to travel the length of the strip. Expand this to various lengths of both distance and time.

X. Discussion

1. Which paper towel is the best buy?
2. Why do some towels absorb faster?
3. Does texture make a difference?
4. Does price give a clue to quality?
5. Does a softer-textured towel absorb faster?
6. Why is there a difference between 1- and 2-ply towels?
7. Which towel surprised you most? Why?
8. How have TV advertisements affected your thinking about which paper towel is best?

XI. Extensions

1. Compare wet strengths, dry strengths.
2. Test with other liquids: milk, oil, ketchup, etc.
3. Test your time estimate from the distance formula work above.

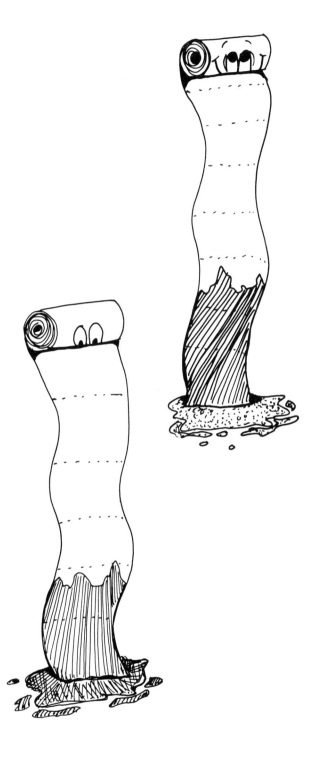

PAPER CAPER

"SPILL MORE" TO THE RESCUE

"MOUNTY IS QUICKER"!

Are all paper towels Created Equal?

This is a job for "MobSquad"!

PREDICTION:

Table of Information

Brand	Plys	thickness	price per roll	sq.ft./m² per roll	seconds to reach 5cm			Average of trials	price per m²	×	cost efficiency = index
					Trial 1	Trial 2	Trial 3				
			$	/							
				/							
				/							
				/							
				/							
				/							
				/							
				/							
				/							
				/							
				/							

Round all decimals to hundredths. To change sq. ft. to m² use the ratio 1 sq. ft. : .0929 m²

CONCLUSIONS:

PAPER CAPER

Rate of Absorption Graph

From the "average of trials" column on the table of information sheet, make a bar graph showing the time each brand of paper towel took to reach the 5cm line. Begin with the 1 ply towels, then all the 2 ply towels, then any 3 ply towels. At the top of the graph, draw a vertical line separating each group.

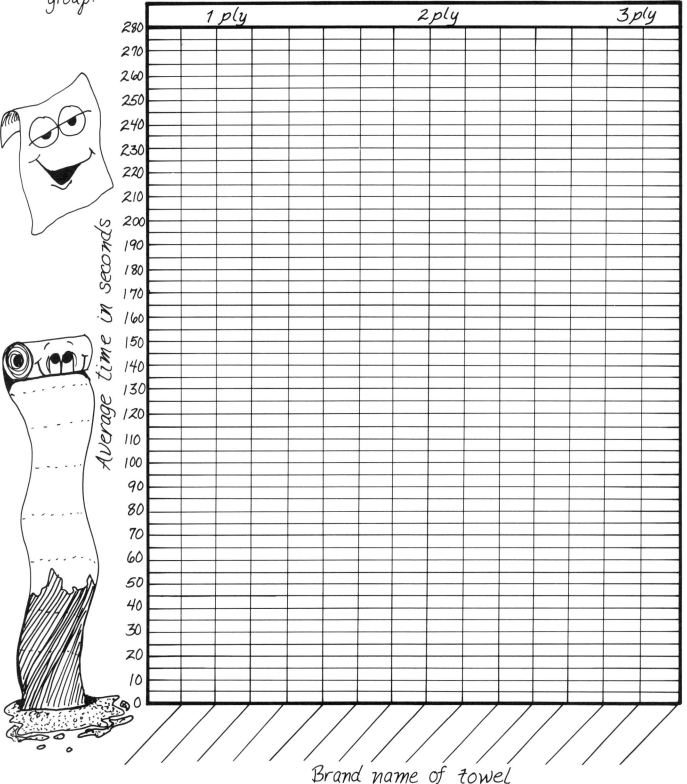

Brand name of towel

49

PAPER CAPER

PRICE COMPARISON GRAPH

Use the "price per m²" column from your table of information sheet to complete this bar graph to compare brands of paper towels.

Begin with the least expensive brand and proceed to the most expensive.

COST EFFICIENCY GRAPH

Construct a line graph using the cost efficiency index from your table of information sheet to rank the paper towels from smallest index number to largest.

The larger the index the less cost efficient the towel.

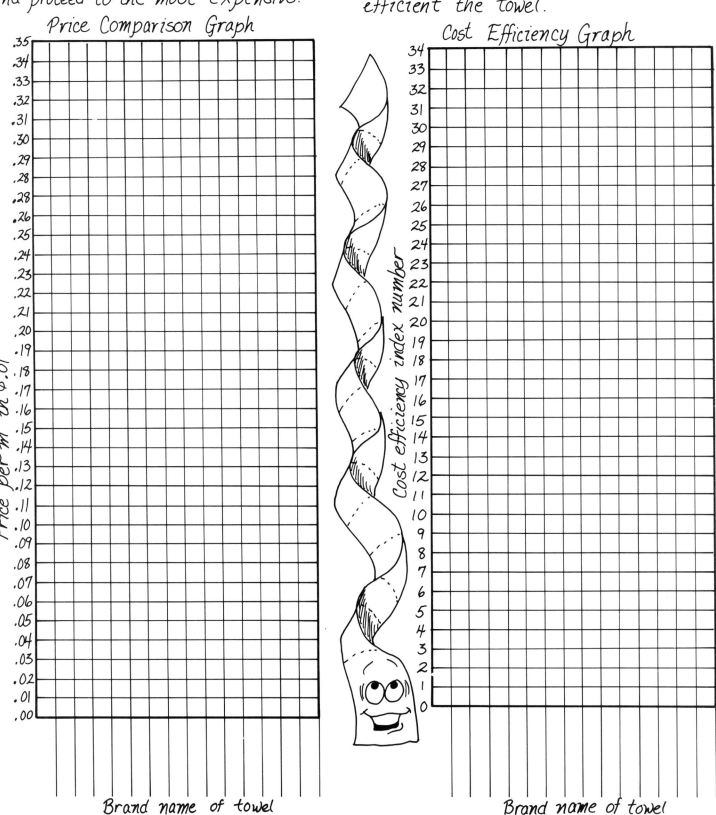

Price Comparison Graph

Price per m² in $.01

Brand name of towel

Cost Efficiency Graph

Cost efficiency index number

Brand name of towel

    © 1987 AIMS Education Foundation

PAPER CAPER II.

I. Topic Area
Absorption Capacity

II. Introductory Statement
Students will become aware of the absorption capacity of various brands of paper towels.

III. Math Skills
a. Ranking
b. Finding percent
c. Finding mass

Science Processes
a. Observing
b. Estimating
c. Recording data

IV. Materials
1 sheet of each brand of paper towel tested in "Paper Caper I"
Metric scale with masses
1 shallow pan for water
Stop watch or second hand on a clock
Student worksheet

V. Key Question
"Which paper towel absorbs the greatest percentage of water?"

VI. Background Information
"The Paper Caper I" should have already been done to familiarize students with the kinds of things they will be working with, as well as the information for the columns headed "plys," "thickness" and "price per m²." The drip time must be the same, and performed the same way, for every towel being tested. Dry the pan of the scale after each wet mass taken. To find the percent of increase divide the "amount of increase" by the "dry mass" and multiply by 100. The greater the number in "absorption efficiency" column the better the towel based on price and performance.

VII. Management Suggestions
To involve more of the class than "The Paper Caper I," students can work in pairs so that twice as many students as paper towels tested can be included. While one student handles the submersion of the towel, the other can time the drip period. Both can be involved in the weighing process. It would be best to dip the towel in a container that is at least as wide as the towel being submersed (about 30 cm wide). Note: a food service tray works well.

VIII. Procedure
1. With students working in pairs, weigh the entire paper towel to find out its dry weight. Record on student worksheet.
2. Submerse the entire towel in water. When it is completely saturated, lift it above the pan and allow it to drip for 30 seconds.
3. Weigh the saturated towel and record the mass.
4. Under "Conclusions," have the students rank at least the last six or so, so that they would have some shopping knowledge.

IX. What the Students Will Do
1. Record plys, thickness, and price per square meter from "The Paper Caper I" student worksheet.
2. Observe the procedure and record both dry and wet weights on the student worksheet, page 30.
3. Subtract to find the amount of increase and record.
4. Find the percent of increase and record.
5. Divide the "amount of increase" by the "price per m²" (round to the nearest tenth) and put the result in "absorption efficiency" column on student worksheet.
6. Draw conclusions about the best 5 or 6 paper towels. Rank from best absorbers toward those not as good.

X. Discussion
1. What makes a paper towel good?
2. Can one paper towel be considered good for one job and not another? Give examples.
3. Which of these most effects your choice of which towel to use: appearance, size, thickness, brand name, advertisement, price, other?
4. Does thickness definitely affect its capacity?
5. Is price a clue to capacity?
6. Is softer better?
7. Do 2-ply towels hold twice as much as 1-ply?

XI. Extensions
1. Test with other liquids: milk, oil, vinegar, 409.
2. Test using different temperature water.

PAPER CAPER II.

Brand	plys	thickness	dry mass	Saturated mass	Amount of increase	% of increase	price per m²	absorption efficiency

Absorption efficiency = Amount of increase ÷ Price per m²

Conclusions: _____

I. Topic Area
Increased size of bread dough will be measured.

II. Introductory Statement
Over a four (4) hour period the bread dough will be monitored and measured before and after baking.

III. Math Skills
a. Measuring; linear, volume, mass
b. Comparing differences
c. Timing—clock
d. Estimating

Science Processes
a. Observing
b. Reporting observations
c. Hypothesizing
d. Following sequential directions

IV. Materials
Any bread recipe and the ingredients it calls for
Foil muffin cups or 4 Pyrex custard dishes or 4 muffin tins (with 6 compartments)
Bowls (large and small)
Measuring cups, spoons
Liter container with ml markings
Scale, weights
Centimeter rulers
Wooden spoons
Student worksheet

V. Key Question
"What effect does rising time have on yeast breads?"

VI. Background Information
Yeast is just one of several agents which are used to make bread rise. Salt, soda, and potatoes were used by the pioneers. Quick breads utilize baking powder as a rising agent.

Yeast is a plant. It consumes sugar and releases alcohol and carbon dioxide (CO_2 gas). Warm water and a warm environment causes the yeast to grow faster. When the bread is baking the yeast continues to grow, resulting in spaces in the finished product. The yeast plant is killed by extreme heat. At that point growth of the product stops. The alcohol that is a result of this fermentation process is "burned off" and is no longer in the baked product.

VII. Management Suggestions
1. Because this investigation could be messy, you may want to demonstrate the bread-making process.
2. Students with freshly washed hands can knead the dough to achieve elasticity.
3. Bread, when properly prepared, needs about 2 hours for the first rising. This is dependent on the warmth of the area where your bread dough is rising.
4. The aroma of freshly baked bread is very stimulating. Shape the bread that is not used for the investigation into rolls or a loaf for baking. Everyone will want to sample it.
5. Once the bread dough is made, the class can resume normal activities. It takes about 20-30 minutes to prepare the dough and explain the process.
6. Baking can be done in a school oven, toaster oven, or fry pan with a rack inside.

VIII. Procedures
1. Prepare bread dough and knead it.
2. Weigh ½ liter of the dough. Record data.
3. Place the dough in a buttered or oiled bowl. Be sure the surface of the dough has a thin oil film, too.
4. You may wish to use transparent plastic liter cubes to let the dough rise. If they are filled half full, it is easy to record when the dough has doubled in size. If these are not available, the students will need to estimate by marking the bowl on the outside where the dough was originally and where it will be when doubled.
5. Cover the bowl and put it in a warm, draft-free environment.
6. Check the dough every 30-45 minutes.
7. Weigh the dough when it has doubled in volume. The liter cube is a real help here as you first weighed .5 of a liter of dough and you now will weigh 1 liter of dough. Record the data.

IX. What the Students Will Do

1. After the dough has been punched down, the children can rub each pan or muffin liner lightly with salad oil or melted margarine or butter.

2. Weigh 50 grams of bread dough. Form it into a smooth ball and place it in one of the prepared pans.

3. Bake the first sample immediately.

4. Place the other 50-gram samples in a warm, draft-free environment.

5. At 30-minute intervals bake remaining samples.

6. After each sample is cool:
   a. Weigh it
   b. Place the roll in a plastic baggie and seal it, then measure the volume by water displacement.
   c. Cut the roll from top to bottom and measure the depth of the roll
   d. Enter all data on the record sheets.

7. When the remainder of your dough has doubled in volume, bake the remaining rolls.

8. Eat rolls with "Better Butter."

X. Discussion

1. Was there a difference in the weight of the bread dough before rising, during rising, and after it was baked?

2. Which roll did you think was best? Why?

3. Which roll had the greatest volume? Why?

4. Why does it take such a long time to make bread?

XI. Extension

1. Make other types of breads such as wheat, rye, or raisin bread.

2. Compare quick breads with yeast breads.

3. Find other recipes that contain bread as a main ingredient.

4. Conduct a water displacement exercise using a yeast solution with sugar to find out how much gas is released.

5. Experiment with making other yeast starters such as sourdough and "Herman."

6. Meal Plan
   Salad Daze
   Fraction Soup
   Bread with Better Butter
   Fondue Fractions

YEAST HIGH RISERS

SAMPLES	#1	#2	#3	#4
RISING TIME	O min.	30 min.	60 min.	90 min.
DOUGH WEIGHT	50 g	50 g	50 g	50 g
WEIGHT AFTER BAKING	g	g	g	g
DEPTH OF BREAD	cm	cm	cm	cm
✳ VOLUME OF BREAD	cm³	cm³	cm³	cm³

DEPTH

1 cubic centimeter = 1 milliliter (ml)   cm³ = cubic centimeter

✳ To find the volume of the baked bread, put the roll in a water tight plastic bag. Tie a knot after all the air has been forced out.

Submerge the bag in a litre container with 500 ml (cm³) of water. The difference between the new water level and 500ml is the **volume** of the bread.

A pencil will help submerge the bread

VOLUME COMPUTATION →

1.	cm³	2.	cm³
	− 500 cm³		− 500 cm³
	cm³		cm³
3.	cm³	4.	cm³
	− 500 cm³		− 500 cm³
	cm³		cm³

My Moldy Garden

I. Topic Area
Examination of mold growth as related to types of bread and ingredients.

II. Introductory Statement
Individual samples of bread will be monitored daily in a longitudinal study of the development of bread mold. The students will learn that not all breads mold at the same rate although the conditions will be the same.

III. Math Skills

a. Measuring surface area, metric
b. Computing surface area and linear measurement

Science Processes

a. Observing
b. Recording data
c. Controlling variables
d. Hypothesizing

IV. Materials
Bread (each student brings his own)
Plastic sandwich bags, 1 per student
Twist ties, 1 per student
Transparent cm grids or metric rulers
Student worksheets
Black construction paper
Staples, tape or glue

V. Key Question
"Does the content of preservative in bread retard mold growth?"

VI. Background Information
Dampness, warmth and the absence of light will yield optimum results in growing molds. The bread provides the food for the mold's growth.

Molds should be handled carefully. *Do not* remove the mold samples from the pastic bags as the spores ("primitive seeds" by which the mold is transported) may spread throughout the classroom. The spores may cause allergic reactions.

In nature, molds are needed to break down substances such as leaves. The results of this is organic matter that enriches the soil. We commonly call much of the organic matter humus or compost.

VII. Management Suggestions
Although each student can conduct this experiment on his own, everything will progress more smoothly with advance preparation. Be sure that each student can bring a slice of bread and a baggie if you wish. Have the students bring a variety of breads such as white, brown, rye, sour dough, tortillas, homemade, or use a sample from your class cooking projects. If the students are unable to bring the bread wrapper to school they will need to copy the ingredients or recipe if it is a homemade bread product.

Make the shade boxes the day before. Using a 9 by 12 inch piece of black construction paper each student can make a box which will sit over his bread sample. Fold 3 cm over on all sides of the paper. Open the paper and crease each corner. Use the crease to keep the 3 cm sides of the paper at 90°

angles to the larger flat surface. Tape the corners. This will form a box which will provide the darkness the bread samples need, as well as added warmth if they are placed in a sunny location. If the samples are to be moved daily, place them on cookie sheets so as to minimize handling the baggies.

IX. What the Students Will Do
1. The day before the investigation is to begin, make shade boxes.
2. If the sample of bread is rectangular or square the student is ready to begin. If not, the student will have to measure and cut his sample to the desired size unless he is familiar with computation of the area of a circle or oval.
3. After the sample is ready, trace its shape on the centimeter grid area of the worksheet. This will give an outline of the sample in which the students can record the growth of their own mold garden.
4. Place a 5 x 5 cm square of damp paper under the slice of bread and put it in the plastic bag. Twist tie it tightly.
5. Place the baggies in a warm place and cover them with the shade boxes. Each student should put his name on the shade box with a piece of masking tape.
6. Observe daily and color in mold growth and graph an estimation of the square centimeters of mold growth. This can easily be done by laying a transparent centimeter grid over the sample and counting the square centimeters. Advanced students may measure and compute each area of mold growth and then add all growth areas to arrive at total surface area of mold growth.
7. The last day of the project the students should record their conclusions as to what affected the growth of their own mold. Before doing this, they will have had many conversations on the differences in the samples and had opportunity to hypothesize as to what could have caused the differences.

X. Discussion
1. Was there a difference in the rate of mold growth?
2. Which samples had the fastest growth?
3. Were there factors which may have caused these differences?
4. Was there more than one type of mold on the samples?
5. How does the addition of preservatives to the bread affect the growth of molds?
6. What can be said of the use of preservatives, shelf life of the product, and storage methods?

XI. Extension
1. Change the variables and repeat the experiment. An example would be to place some bread in the dark and expose another identical piece to the light.
2. Using the same technique, mold can be grown on other items. Oranges, leaves, and cheese are particularly good.
3. Study the use of molds which are beneficial as well as those which are not.

My Moldy Garden

DATE: _____ to _____

INVESTIGATOR: _____

My Moldy Garden

name _____

Medium _____
(Type of Bread)

TYPE OF FLOUR _____

Preservatives (mark one)	yes	no

1. Trace your bread then bag it!
2. Observe your bread every day at the same time.
3. Color the mold growth day by day, using a different color for each day. Use the color order below:

DAY 1.   2.   3.   4.   5.   6.   7.   8.   9.   10.
black- pink—red—green—blue- orange-yellow-purple-lime — gray

My Moldy Garden Data Sheet

Area = length X width

Name of Bread Product: _____

Label Contents or recipe:

1. _____
2. _____
3. _____
4. _____
5. _____
6. _____

7. _____
8. _____
9. _____
10. _____
11. _____
12. _____

✳ Before recording this data, your bread must be put in a baggie and twist tied. Weigh the bread today while it is in the baggie and again at the end of the investigation the same way.

FIRST DAY: _____ (date)   _____ (time)

✳ Weight in grams : _____   cm length _____

Surface Area : _____ cm²   cm wide _____

LAST DAY: _____ (date)   _____ (time)

✳ Weight in grams: _____   cm length _____

Surface Area: _____ cm²   cm wide _____

My Moldy Garden

HOW DOES MY GARDEN GROW?

NAME _____

Graphic isn't it?

Conclusions:

Surface Area of Mold (square centimeters)

15
14
13
12
11
10
9
8
7
6
5
4
3
2
1

1 black
2 pink
3 red
4 green
5 blue
6 orange
7 yellow
8 purple
9 lime
10 gray

JUICY FRUIT

I. Topic Area
Dehydration of fruits and vegetables.

II. Introductory Statement
Students will become aware of the surprising amount of water contained in these foods (at least 50%).

III. Math Skills
a. Finding mass
b. Using ratios
c. Finding percent
d. Graphing

Science Processes
a. Measuring
b. Recording data
c. Interpreting data
d. Observing and generalizing

IV. Materials
A part of, or the entire food to be tested (see student sheet)
Knife
Plastic wrap (Saran, Handiwrap)
Aluminum foil
Gram scale and masses
Oven, any kind (regular, toaster, convection) or dehydrator
Student worksheet

V. Key Question
"How much of these (foods) is water?"

VII. Management Suggestions
1. This investigation can be done in about 45 minutes.
2. Have students work in pairs on each food. If in a departmentalized program, have each food handled by a different period and share results.
3. Because of the difference in ovens each oven should be tested for temperature and time before beginning the investigation.

VIII. Procedure
1. Have a student physically arrange the foods in the order of estimated greatest to least amount of water. Then have each student write his own arrangement on the back. Using the inequality symbol > between each food in the line makes a nice way of ordering, i.e., watermelon > potato > carrot...).
2. After ranking foods, students should estimate the percent of water in each food and record before proceeding.

IX. What the Students Will Do
1. Make an aluminum foil pan from a square of foil one half the width of the roll, 15 cm (6") Note: this will weigh about 1 g.
2. Slice enough food about 3mm thick to cover the bottom of the pan without overlapping.
3. Weigh this pan of food and record in "Beginning Mass" column.
4. Place in warm oven or dehydrator at about 65°C (150°F) and leave about 6 hours (or 24 hours to completely dehydrate). In an oven leave door ajar. This food will not be edible.
5. When dry, remove from oven and weigh again. The difference will be the amount of water lost.
6. Complete the table of information and the graph.
7. Compare your estimated rank with actual ranking.

X. Discussion
1. How much are you paying for water?
2. Why do we leave the door ajar on the oven? Why does the dehydrator have vents? This may lead to discussion of evaporation and water vapor.
3. Which food had the most surprising results?

XI. Extension
1. Compute the price of the water in the foods.
2. Do the investigation using meats.

JUICY FRUIT _____ NAME

DOES THE WATERMELON HAVE THE RIGHT NAME?

HOW MUCH WATER DO YOU THINK ARE IN THESE FRUITS?
ESTIMATE THE PART OR PERCENTAGE FOR EACH:

WATERMELON _____	BANANA _____	POTATO _____
APPLE _____	PEAR _____	SQUASH _____
CARROT _____	TOMATO _____	CELERY _____

FIND THE MASS (g) OF A SAMPLE OF EACH OF THESE FRUITS.
THEN PLACE THE SAMPLES IN A WARM OVEN (95° CELSIUS) AND LEAVE FOR
8-10 HOURS. WEIGH EACH SAMPLE AGAIN (AFTER EXPOSURE TO HEAT) TO FIND THE
AMOUNT OF WATER EACH LOST. RECORD THE RESULTS IN THE TABLE.

SAMPLE	BEGINNING MASS (g)	FINAL MASS AFTER DRYING (g)	LOSS OF MASS (g) (WATER)	LOSS OF MASS / BEGINNING MASS (RATIO)	PERCENTAGE OF WATER
WATERMELON					
APPLE					
CARROT					
BANANA					
PEAR					
TOMATO					
POTATO					
SQUASH					
CELERY					

CONSTRUCT A BAR GRAPH SHOWING THE PERCENTAGE OF WATER IN EACH FRUIT.

SAMPLE	0%	10%	20%	30%	40%	50%	60%	70%	80%	90%	100%
WATERMELON											
APPLE											
CARROT											
BANANA											
PEAR											
TOMATO											
POTATO											
SQUASH											
CELERY											

Dry It Out

THERE IS NO STUDENT WORKSHEET FOR THIS INVESTIGATION

I. Topic Area
Dehydration of foods for storage.

II. Introductory Statement
Students will discover this age-old method of preserving food for future use.

III. Math Skills / Science Processes

Math Skills
a. Measuring masses
b. Finding percent

Science Processes
a. Observing

IV. Materials
Fruits to be dried
Drying trays—wood, stainless steel, window screen
Cheese cloth
Knife

V. Key Question
How effective is dehydration as a form of preservation of fruits and vegetables?

VI. Background Information
The goal of drying foods is to reduce its moisture content to between 5 to 25 percent so that bacteria which causes decay cannot survive. Drying foods will reduce the original mass. Food value of dried food is preserved over that of freezing or canning and has no expiration date. Sun energy, when used instead of an oven or a dehydrator, is absolutely free. For immediate use it is not necessary to sulfur or treat food. Sulfuring is done as a color preservative. Dips, such as lemon, honey or ascorbic acid are used for the same purpose. Never put sulfured food in an oven or a dehydrator. Fruits are dry when leather or crisp and not wet or moist when squeezed.

VII. Management Suggestions
Since time and equipment are factors in this investigation, it will probably be done by the students at home. If you have a convection oven which you can bring to school it can be done as a school activity.

VIII. Procedures
1. Select whatever foods are available for drying. Fruits make better snacks than vegetables. Vegetables such as carrots, celery and tomatoes are interesting, if not easy to snack on. Bananas are always available and fit in with "Waste Not Want Not" in this book and "The Big Banana Peel" in Book 1. Other available fruits are apples and grapes in the fall and in the spring there might be some early apricots, peaches or plums.
2. Select fully ripe fruit.

Sun Dry Method
Leave grapes whole either in bunches or separated.
Place on tray, cover with cheese cloth, dry on one side, turn and dry the other side. (6-10 days)
Fruits should be covered at night to protect them from dew.

Oven/Dehydrator Method
Grapes—not recommended because of the skin, it takes too long. Better outdoors.
All fruits and vegetables should be sliced to 1/8 inch and spread in single layer on tray. Dry at about 49°C (120°F) for 8-12 hours.

3. Meats: except for making jerkys, all meats should be cooked first. Leftover meats (poultry, beef, ham and lamb) are good choices for drying. Trim off all fat, since it will turn rancid in time. Cut into even cubes about 1 cm.

Sun Dry Method
Spread a single layer on trays, dry until hard. (2-3 days)

Oven/Dehydrator Method
Dry at 60°C (140°F) for about 6 hours.

4. Jerky: Use very lean chuck or round steak. Trim off all traces of fat. Freeze until firm enough to cut thin slices 3 mm (1/8 inch) across grain of meat. Cut into strips of 2-3 cm (1-1½ inch) wide. Marinate over night (see recipe), then place on trays and dry in oven or dehydrator at 140°F until strips splinter when bent (about 18-24 hours). Sun drying is not recommended.

X. Discussion
Discuss value of dehydration as a way of preserving foods for future use. Compare it with freezing and canning for ease and storage space. Discuss energy use in various methods.

BEEF MARINADE
59 ml (¼ c.) Worcestershire sauce
59 ml (¼ c.) soy sauce
1 T.   tomato sauce
1 T.   vinegar
1 t.   sugar
¼ t.   dried garlic, chopped
¼ t.   dried onion, chopped
1 t.   salt
Combine in blender. Pour over meat strips in shallow pan. Refrigerate over night, drain and dry as instructed under Procedures, part 4.

63

I. Topic Area
Nutrition

II. Introductory Statement
The students will discover their daily nutritional needs resulting in design of their own perfect sandwich.

III. Math Skills
a. Problem solving
b. Sorting
c. Writing fractional parts

Science Processes
a. Observing
b. Classifying
c. Recording data
d. Predicting

IV. Materials
Chart of food groups
Student worksheets

VII. Management Suggestions
1. This project is not limited to one grade level or any size group.
2. This project should be divided into several sessions.
3. Time limit—approximately 3 one-hour sessions.

VIII. Procedure

Session 1
1. Without any previous discussion, have each student write down their opinion or description of a perfect sandwich.
2. Have each student tell what the word "perfect" means to them.
3. Make a student list on the chalkboard of all possible ingredients for a sandwich.

Session 2
1. Review the basic food groups with the class.
2. Classify all ingredients into the four basic food groups.
3. Discuss the daily requirements for each food group.

Session 3
1. Decide on the amount of each food group needed for a perfect sandwich.
2. Record your ingredients for your perfect sandwich.
3. Complete chart.
4. Evaluate your final choices of ingredients.

X. Discussion
1. What are the basic food group requirements for a day?
2. Is the perfect sandwich the same for everyone?
3. How many perfect sandwiches can you list?

XI. Extension
1. The perfect sandwich could be determined by food groups with emphasis on calories.
2. Students could make their perfect sandwich and bring it to school for a special event.
3. Decide which fast food sandwich (taco, sandwich, burger, etc.) is the most nearly perfect.

THE "Perfect Sandwich"

INGREDIENT	FOOD GROUP	NUMBER OF SERVINGS	DAILY SERVINGS REQUIRED	FRACTION OF DAILY REQUIREMENT
1.				
2.				
3.				
4.				
5.				
6.				
7.				
8.				
9.				
10.				
11.				
12.				
13.				
14.				

65

Daily Food Guide

I. Topic Area
Nutrition and making wise choices in a balanced diet.

II. Introductory Statement
The students will record their individual food choices at home and at school as well as recording calories. The culmination will be a private conference with the teacher to discuss the results.

III. Math Skills
a. Adding
b. Estimating of food quantities
c. Averaging

Science Processes
a. Recording data

IV. Materials
Calorie charts or booklets (The students may share 2 or 3 copies)
Student worksheets
A construction paper folder for each student

V. Key Questions
"Do I make wise nutritional choices?"
"Do I consume an adequate amount of calories for good health?"

VI. Background Information
Within the calorie books you use or your health book will be the calorie requirements for different age groups as well as height and weight charts. These are only to be used as a guide. Most weight charts list the ideal weights at a lower estimate than what some authorities consider to be normal. Nevertheless, it is important for young adults to learn that many of their favorite snacks are loaded with calories that slowly add pounds to their frames.

VII. Management Suggestions
Once the worksheets are explained, it would be wise to devote time to the confidentiality of this project. Assure your students that the results of this study are for them and not a part of a future general discussion. Private conferences will be used to go over the report. At this time the student may relay to the teacher his/her findings about his/her choices.

VIII. Procedures
1. After explaining the meaning of the project, you will want to establish a few guidelines for collecting data.
2. Within the construction paper folders, the students will have adequate worksheets for daily recording. They may take these folders home, as the majority of their meals and snacks are at home.
3. Looking up the calorie contents of these foods can be done at school at any time during the day that is convenient for your schedule. It is important that this be a private activity.
4. This is not a study of ethnic diets. Each culture has its own preference for each food group. The overweight student will certainly be grateful for a private study, and may be able to change his habits. For these reasons we feel that individual conferences are best at the conclusion of the investigative week.

IX. What the Students Will Do
1. Each day the students will enter the foods and calories of the foods they have eaten.
2. Each day will have a total number of calories.
3. Each day will be graphed according to total calories consumed.
4. Each student will be responsible for drawing his own conclusions before the individual conference and having all data complete.

X. Discussion
1. How do you feel about the diet you have selected?
2. Do you have adequate energy from the foods you eat?
3. Have your choices changed during this investigation? Why? How?
4. Has this investigation been helpful to you? Why or why not?

XI. Extension
1. Compute the amount of exercise that is needed to burn off the calories that were consumed each day.
2. Prepare a meal plan that includes good choices for you and your family.

Daily Food Guide

Follow The Food Guide Every Day

Milk Group

Some for Everyone!

1 serving = 1 cup milk

Children under 9 : 2 – 3 cups
Children 9-12 : 3 or more
Teenagers : 4 or more
Adults : 2 or more
Pregnant Women : 3 or more
Nursing Mothers : 4 or more

Cheese may be used for part of the milk

Meat Group

2 or more Servings

Count as a serving: 2 or 3 ounces of cooked lean meat-such as a hamburger, a chicken leg, or a fish. Also 2 eggs, or 1 cup cooked dry beans or peas or 4 tablespoons peanut butter.

Vegetable-Fruit Group

4 or more Servings

Count as 1 serving ½ cup raw or cooked, or 1 portion such as ~~~~~~ or 👃 or 🥣 or 🍎.

Bread-Cereal Group

4 or more servings

Count as 1 serving :
1 slice of bread or 1 buscuit or 1 ounce ready to eat cereal or ½ – ¾ cup cooked cereal – cornmeal, grits, macaroni, rice, or spaghetti.

7-DAY EATING CHART

Name ——

How well do you eat?

Place a check ✓ for each serving that you eat per day

SERVINGS OF FOOD

	DAY 1	DAY 2	DAY 3	DAY 4	DAY 5	DAY 6	DAY 7	WEEKLY TOTAL SERVINGS	AVERAGE DAILY SERVINGS
MILK GROUP									
PROTEIN GROUP									
VEGETABLE FRUIT GROUP									
BREAD-CEREAL GROUP									

Here's how many servings of each food group that you need to have a well-balanced food day.

PROTEIN GROUP - 2 servings

BREAD-CEREAL GROUP- 4 servings

MILK GROUP - 4 servings

VEGETABLE-FRUIT GROUP-4 servings

RECOMMENDED DAILY ALLOWANCES
CALORIC INTAKE

	AGE	WEIGHT (POUNDS)	(KILOGRAMS)	HEIGHT (INCHES)	(CENTIMETERS)	CALORIES (ENERGY)
KIDS	1-3	28	13	34	86	1300
	4-6	44	120	44	112	1800
	7-10	66	30	54	137	2400
MALES	11-14	97	44	63	160	2800
	15-18	134	61	69	175	3000
	19-22	147	67	69	175	3000
	23-50	154	70	69	175	2700
	51⁺	154	70	69	175	2400
FEMALES	11-14	97	44	62	157	2400
	15-18	119	54	65	165	2100
	19-22	128	58	65	165	2100
	23-50	128	58	65	165	2000
	51⁺	128	58	65	165	1800

DATE_____   NAME _____

Daily Food Intake

Meal	Item	Amount	Calories
Breakfast			
		Total	Total
Lunch			
		Total	Total
Dinner			
		Total	Total
Snacks			
		Total	Total

Calories for the Week Sheet

Sunday
Breakfast
Lunch
Dinner
Snacks

Total _____

Monday
Breakfast
Lunch
Dinner
Snacks

Total _____

Tuesday
Breakfast
Lunch
Dinner
Snacks

Total _____

Wednesday
Breakfast
Lunch
Dinner
Snacks

Total _____

Thursday
Breakfast
Lunch
Dinner
Snacks

Total _____

Friday
Breakfast
Lunch
Dinner
Snacks

Total _____

Saturday
Breakfast
Lunch
Dinner
Snacks

Total _____

Total
Sunday
Monday
Tuesday
Wednesday
Thursday
Friday
Saturday

Average Daily Calories

Total for the Week

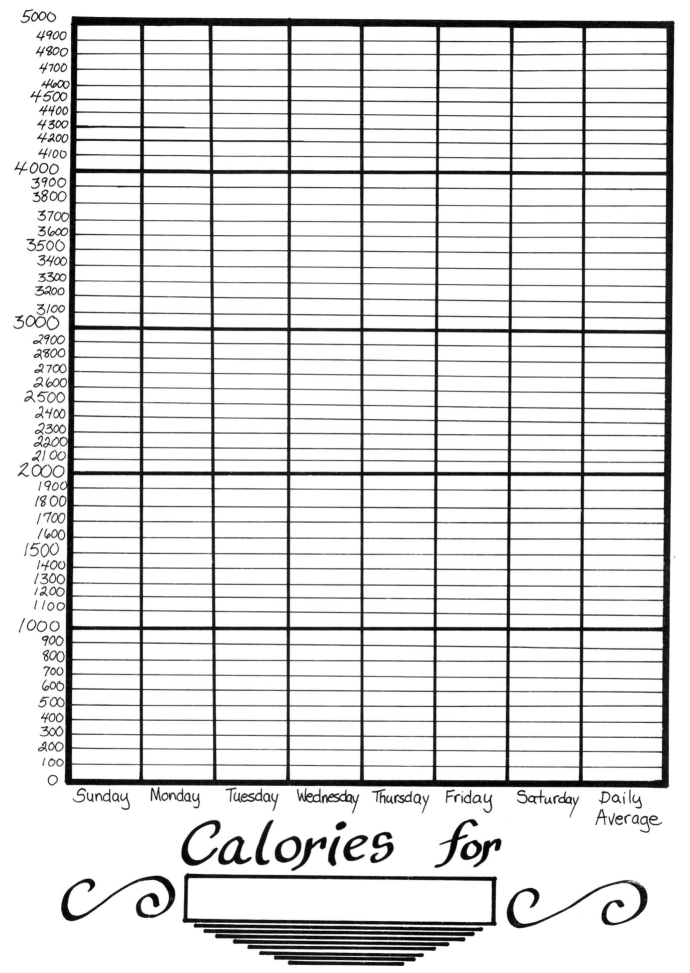

	Sunday	Monday	Tuesday	Wednesday	Thursday	Friday	Saturday	Daily Average

Calories for

Cafeteria Critique

I. Topic Area
A longitudinal study of cafeteria lunches and the food groups they contain.

II. Introductory Statement
We will conduct a study of what is being served in the school cafeteria and the types of foods and meals that children enjoy.

III. Math Skills
a. Finding percent
b. Counting
c. Adding
d. Graphing
e. Rounding decimals

Science Processes
a. Collecting data
b. Classifying
c. Interpreting data

IV. Materials
Paper and pencils
School lunch menu
Student worksheets

V. Key Question
What percentage of our school lunches are enjoyed? What percentage of our school lunches comes from each food group?

VI. Background Information
Under government regulations each school lunch must have:

MILK—½ pint of milk, unflavored lowfat milk, non-fat milk, or buttermilk.

MEAT—2 ounces of meat, poultry, fish, cheese; 2 eggs or 1 cup cooked dry beans; or any combination equal in quantity.

FRUIT/VEGETABLES—¾ of a cup of vegetables and fruit; (must include at least 2).

BREAD OR ALTERNATE—8 servings per week of bread made with whole grain or enriched flour or ½ cup rice or enriched pasta products.

A study of this type should illustrate the fact that the school lunch program is indeed balanced. If your school has a great deal of waste, this investigation may help curb the problem.

Some schools have a lunch program where each student chooses what s/he wants on his/her tray. By modifying this plan you can analyze their choices rather than what they are given.

VII. Management Suggestion
Although a study of this type takes 2 weeks to complete if you are using it according to the lesson plan, it can be done in 1 hour if you use a menu rather than actually doing it day by day. Each student could decide which meals they like best by reading rather than tasting.

This investigation should not take more than 10 minutes daily. Each student should keep his Cafeteria Critique in a folder to insure a clean copy after 10 school days. The tenth day of data collecting should take about 45 minutes due to the computation.

Some students may have difficulty with the circle graph. It is helpful for these students to think of the circle as a clock face. Instead of 60 minute markings our clock must have 100 marks to represent 100%. When they have computed their percentages all that is needed is to count the notches to represent the percentage needed. Younger students may choose to use a cut and paste method with 5 "clocks", eventually mounted as one circle graph.

VIII. Procedure
1. On the first day explain that the class will be doing a critique on cafeteria meals. Students who bring cold lunches may wish to critique their own lunches in the same manner. They may wish to indicate this on their data sheet.
2. Explain the tally system.
3. On day ten, total all tallies, compute percentages and construct the circle graph.

IX. What the Students Will Do
1. Tally each food item on their menu.
2. Evaluate the lunch by making a happy, sad, or just O.K. face by each day's number.
3. On day ten they will do parts 1 and 2 as well as all computation and graphing.
4. Discussion and questions.

X. Discussion Questions
1. What food groups were represented the most?
2. What food groups were represented the least?
3. Which meals are most favored by students?
4. Were all food groups represented according to government standards?

XI. Extension
1. Compute class averages for 😊, 😐, 😟 to determine class favorites. Conduct a school study to see if your class is representative of the school population.
2. Make a top 10 menu that is full of things kids love. All meals must be balanced.

Cafeteria Critique

_____ Name

MEATS   MILK   FRUITS & VEGETABLES   BREAD & CEREALS   NO FOOD VALUE

Did you enjoy your lunch today?

Draw a ∪ for yes

Draw a ∩ for no

Draw a ⊢ if it was just O.K.

DAY	MEATS	MILK	FRUITS & VEGETABLES	BREAD & CEREALS	NO FOOD VALUE
1					
2					
3					
4					
5					
6					
7					
8					
9					
10					

TOTALS ___ ___ ___ ___ ___

∪ What % of the meals did you enjoy? _____ %
∩ What % of the meals did you dislike? _____ %
⊢ What % of the meals were just O.K.? _____ %

example: ☺ = 5 $\frac{5}{10} = \frac{n}{100}$

$n = 50\%$

Number of:

_____ meat servings
_____ milk servings
_____ fruit & vegetable servings
_____ bread & cereal servings
_____ no food value

TOTAL SERVINGS
(count all tallies)

_____

Cafeteria Critique

RATION RATIO = $\dfrac{\text{\# FOOD GROUP SERVINGS}}{\text{TOTAL SERVINGS}}$

Example

$\dfrac{15 \text{ milk servings}}{70 \text{ total servings}}$

$\dfrac{15}{70} = \dfrac{n}{100}$

$n = 21.428 \%$ milk

Per Cent

MY C. C. G.

(Cafeteria Circle Graph)

Meats _____ = $\dfrac{n}{100}$

$n =$ _____ %

FRUITS & VEGETABLES

_____ = $\dfrac{n}{100}$

$n =$ _____ %

BREADS & CEREALS

 _____ = $\dfrac{n}{100}$

$n =$ _____ %

NO FOOD VALUE

_____ = $\dfrac{n}{100}$

$n =$ _____ %

MILK

_____ = $\dfrac{n}{100}$

$n =$ _____ %

FUN WITH FOODS   75   © 1987 AIMS Education Foundation

The AIMS Program

AIMS is the acronym for "**A**ctivities **I**ntegrating **M**athematics and **S**cience." Such integration enriches learning and makes it meaningful and holistic. AIMS began as a project of Fresno Pacific College to integrate the study of mathematics and science in grades K-9, but has since expanded to include language arts, social studies, and other disciplines.

AIMS is a continuing program of the non-profit AIMS Education Foundation. It had its inception in a National Science Foundation funded program whose purpose was to explore the effectiveness of integrating mathematics and science. The project directors in cooperation with eighty elementary classroom teachers devoted two years to a thorough field-testing of the results and implications of integration.

The approach met with such positive results that the decision was made to launch a program to create instructional materials incorporating this concept. Despite the fact that thoughtful educators have long recommended an integrative approach, very little appropriate material was available in 1981 when the project began. A series of writing projects have ensued and today the AIMS Education Foundation is committed to continue the creation of new integrated activities on a permanent basis.

The AIMS program is funded through the sale of this developing series of books and proceeds from the Foundation's endowment. All net income from program and products flows into a trust fund administered by the AIMS Education Foundation. Use of these funds is restricted to support of research, development, and publication of new materials. Writers donate all their rights to the Foundation to support its on-going program. No royalties are paid to the writers.

The rationale for integration lies in the fact that science, mathematics, language arts, social studies, etc., are integrally interwoven in the real world from which it follows that they should be similarly treated in the classroom where we are preparing students to live in that world. Teachers who use the AIMS program give enthusiastic endorsement to the effectiveness of this approach.

Science encompasses the art of questioning, investigating, hypothesizing, discovering and communicating. Mathematics is the language that provides clarity, objectivity, and understanding. The language arts provide us powerful tools of communication. Many of the major contemporary societal issues stem from advancements in science and must be studied in the context of the social sciences. Therefore, it is timely that all of us take seriously a more holistic mode of educating our students. This goal motivates all who are associated with the AIMS Program. We invite you to join us in this effort.

Meaningful integration of knowledge is a major recommendation coming from the nation's professional science and mathematics associations. The American Association for the Advancement of Science in *Science for All Americans* strongly recommends the integration of mathematics, science, and technology. The National Council of Teachers of Mathematics places strong emphasis on applications of mathematics such as are found in science investigations. AIMS is fully aligned with these recommendations.

Extensive field testing of AIMS investigations confirms these beneficial results.
1. Mathematics becomes more meaningful, hence more useful, when it is applied to situations that interest students.
2. The extent to which science is studied and understood is increased, with a significant economy of time, when mathematics and science are integrated.
3. There is improved quality of learning and retention, supporting the thesis that learning which is meaningful and relevant is more effective.
4. Motivation and involvement are increased dramatically as students investigate real-world situations and participate actively in the process.

We invite you to become part of this classroom teacher movement by using an integrated approach to learning and sharing any suggestions you may have. The AIMS Program welcomes you!

AIMS Education Foundation Programs

A Day With AIMS

Intensive one-day workshops are offered to introduce educators to the philosophy and rationale of AIMS. Participants will discuss the methodology of AIMS and the strategies by which AIMS principles may be incorporated into curriculum. Each participant will take part in a variety of hands-on AIMS investigations to gain an understanding of such aspects as the scientific/mathematical content, classroom management, and connections with other curricular areas. The *A Day With AIMS* workshops may be offered anywhere in the United States. Necessary supplies and take-home materials are usually included in the enrollment fee.

AIMS One-Week Workshops

Throughout the nation, AIMS offers many one-week workshops each year, usually in the summer. Each workshop lasts five days and includes at least 30 hours of AIMS hands-on instruction. Participants are grouped according to the grade level(s) in which they are interested. Instructors are members of the AIMS Instructional Leadership Network. Supplies for the activities and a generous supply of take-home materials are included in the enrollment fee. Sites are selected on the basis of applications submitted by educational organizations. If chosen to host a workshop, the host agency agrees to provide specified facilities and cooperate in the promotion of the workshop. The AIMS Education Foundation supplies workshop materials as well as the travel, housing, and meals for instructors.

AIMS One-Week Perspectives Workshops

Each summer, Fresno Pacific College offers AIMS one-week workshops on the campus of Fresno Pacific College in Fresno, California. AIMS Program Directors and highly qualified members of the AIMS National Leadership Network serve as instructors.

The Science Festival and the Festival of Mathematics

Each summer, Fresno Pacific College offers a Science Festival and a Festival of Mathematics. These two-week festivals have gained national recognition as inspiring and challenging experiences, giving unique opportunities to experience hands-on mathematics and science in topical and grade-level groups. Guest faculty includes some of the nation's most highly regarded mathematics and science educators. Supplies and take-home materials are included in the enrollment fee.

The AIMS Instructional Leadership Program

This is an AIMS staff development program seeking to prepare facilitators for leadership roles in science/math education in their home districts or regions. Upon successful completion of the program, trained facilitators become members of the AIMS Instructional Leadership Network, qualified to conduct AIMS workshops, teach AIMS in-service courses for college credit, and serve as AIMS consultants. Intensive training is provided in mathematics, science, process and thinking skills, workshop management, and other relevant topics.

College Credit and Grants

Those who participate in workshops may often qualify for college credit. If the workshop takes place on the campus of Fresno Pacific College, that institution may grant appropriate credit. If the workshop takes place off-campus, arrangements can sometimes be made for credit to be granted by another college or university. In addition, the applicant's home school district is often willing to grant in-service or professional development credit. Many educators who participate in AIMS workshops are recipients of various types of educational grants, either local or national. Nationally known foundations and funding agencies have long recognized the value of AIMS mathematics and science workshops to educators. The AIMS Education Foundation encourages educators interested in attending or hosting workshops to explore the possibilities suggested above. Although the Foundation strongly supports such interest, it reminds applicants that they have the primary responsibility for fulfilling *current* requirements.

For current information regarding the programs described above, please complete the following:

Information Request

Please send current information on the items checked:

____ *Basic Information Packet* on AIMS materials   ____ *AIMS One-Week Perspectives Workshops*
____ *Festival of Mathematics*   ____ *AIMS One-Week Workshops*
____ *Science Festival*   ____ Hosting information for *A Day With AIMS* workshops
____ *AIMS Instructional Leadership Program*   ____ Hosting information for *A Week With AIMS* workshops

Name _____ Phone _____

Address _____
            Street   City   State   Zip

AIMS Program Publications

GRADES K-4 SERIES
Bats Incredible
Brinca de Alegria Hacia la Primavera con las Matemáticas y Ciencias
Cáete de Gusto Hacia el Otoño con la Matemáticas y Ciencias
Fall Into Math and Science
Glide Into Winter With Math and Science
Hardhatting in a Geo-World
Jaw breakers and Heart Thumpers (Revised Edition, 1995)
Overhead and Underfoot (Revised Edition, 1994)
Patine al Invierno con Matemáticas y Ciencias
Popping With Power (Revised Edition, 1994)
Primariamente Física (Revised Edition, 1994)
Primariamente Plantas
Primarily Physics (Revised Edition, 1994)
Primarily Plants
Sense-able Science
Spring Into Math and Science

GRADES K-6 SERIES
Budding Botanist
Critters
El Bonanista Principiante
Mostly Magnets
Ositos Nada Más
Primarily Bears
Principalmente Imanes
Water Precious Water

GRADES 5-9 SERIES
Conexiones Eléctricas
Down to Earth
Electrical Connections
Finding Your Bearings (Revised Edition, 1994)
Floaters and Sinkers (Revised Edition, 1995)
From Head to Toe
Fun With Foods
Historical Connections in Mathematics, Volume I
Historical Connections in Mathematics, Volume II
Historical Connections in Mathematics, Volume III
Brick by Brick
Machine Shop
Magnificent Microworld Adventures
Math + Science, A Solution
Our Wonderful World
Out of This World (Revised Edition, 1994)
Pieces and Patterns, A Patchwork in Math and Science
Piezas y Diseños, un Mosaic de Matemáticas y Ciencias
Soap Films and Bubbles
The Sky's the Limit (Revised Edition, 1994)
Through the Eyes of the Explorers: Minds-on Math & Mapping
Off the Wall Science: A Poster Series Revisited
What's Next, Volume I
What's Next, Volume II
What's Next, Volume III

FOR FURTHER INFORMATION WRITE TO:
AIMS Education Foundation • P.O. Box 8120 • Fresno, California 93747-8120

We invite you to subscribe to *AIMS!*

Each issue of *AIMS* contains a variety of material useful to educators at all grade levels. Feature articles of lasting value deal with topics such as mathematical or science concepts, curriculum, assessment, the teaching of process skills, and historical background. Several of the latest AIMS math/science investigations are always included, along with their reproducible activity sheets. As needs direct and space allows, various issues contain news of current developments, such as workshop schedules, activities of the AIMS Instructional Leadership Network, and announcements of upcoming publications.

AIMS is published monthly, August through May. Subscriptions are on an annual basis only. A subscription entered at any time will begin with the next issue, but will also include the previous issues of that volume. Readers have preferred this arrangement because articles and activities within an annual volume are often interrelated.

Please note that an *AIMS* subscription automatically includes duplication rights for one school site for all issues included in the subscription. Many schools build cost-effective library resources with their subscriptions.

YES! I am interested in subscribing to *AIMS*.

Name _____   Home Phone _____

Address _____   City, State, Zip _____

Please send the following volumes (subject to availability):

_____ Volume II (1987-88) $27.50	_____ Volume VII (1992-93) $27.50
_____ Volume III (1988-89) $27.50	_____ Volume VIII (1993-94) $27.50
_____ Volume IV (1989-90) $27.50	_____ Volume IX (1994-95) $27.50
_____ Volume V (1990-91) $27.50	_____ Volume X (1995-96) $30.00
_____ Volume VI (1991-92) $27.50	_____ Volume XI (1996-97) $30.00

_____ Limited offer: Volumes X & XI (1995-96 & 1996-97) $55.00

(Note: Prices may change without notice. For current prices, call (209) 255-4094.)

Check your method of payment:

☐ Check enclosed in the amount of $ _____
☐ Purchase order attached (Please be sure it includes the P.O. number, the authorizing signature, and the position of the authorizing person.)
☐ Credit Card   (Check One)
   ☐ Visa   ☐ MasterCard   Number _____

Amount $ _____   Expiration Date _____

Signature _____   Today's Date _____

Make checks payable to **AIMS Education Foundation.**
Mail to *AIMS* magazine, **P.O. Box 8120, Fresno, CA 93747-8120.**
Phone (209)255-4094 FAX (209)255-6396, Internet address: aimsed@fresno.edu

AIMS Duplication Rights Program

AIMS has received many requests from school districts for the purchase of unlimited duplication rights to AIMS materials. In response, the AIMS Education Foundation has formulated the program outlined below. There is a built-in flexibility which, we trust, will provide for those who use AIMS materials extensively to purchase such rights for either individual activities or entire books.

It is the goal of the AIMS Education Foundation to make its materials and programs available at reasonable cost. All income from the sale of publications and duplication rights is used to support AIMS programs; hence, strict adherence to regulations governing duplication is essential. Duplication of AIMS materials beyond limits set by copyright laws and those specified below is strictly forbidden.

Limited Duplication Rights

Any purchaser of an AIMS book may make up to *200 copies* of any activity in that book for use at *one school site*. Beyond that, rights must be purchased according to the appropriate category.

Unlimited Duplication Rights for Single Activities

An individual or school may purchase the right to make an unlimited number of copies of a single activity. The royalty is $5.00 per activity per school site.

Examples: 3 activities x 1 site x $5.00 = $15.00
9 activities x 3 sites x $5.00 = $135.00

Unlimited Duplication Rights for Entire Books

A school or district may purchase the right to make an unlimited number of copies of a single, *specified* book. The royalty is $20.00 per book per school site. This is in addition to the cost of the book.

Examples: 5 books x 1 site x $20.00 = $100.00
12 books x 10 sites x $20.00 = $2400.00

Magazine/Newsletter Duplication Rights

Members of the AIMS Education Foundation who purchase the *AIMS* magazine/*Newsletter* are hereby granted permission to make up to 200 copies of any portion of it, provided these copies will be used for educational purposes.

Workshop Instructors' Duplication Rights

Workshop instructors may distribute to registered workshop participants a maximum of 100 copies of any article and/or 100 copies of no more than eight activities, provided these six conditions are met:

1. Since all AIMS activities are based upon the *AIMS Model of Mathematics* and the *AIMS Model of Learning*, leaders must include in their presentations an explanation of these two models.
2. Workshop instructors must relate the AIMS activities presented to these basic explanations of the AIMS philosophy of education.
3. The copyright notice must appear on all materials distributed.
4. Instructors must provide information enabling participants to apply for membership in the AIMS Education Foundation or order books from the Foundation.
5. Instructors must inform participants of their limited duplication rights as outlined below.
6. Only student pages may be duplicated.

Written permission must be obtained for duplication beyond the limits listed above. Additional royalty payments may be required.

Workshop Participants' Rights

Those enrolled in workshops in which AIMS student activity sheets are distributed may duplicate a maximum of 35 copies or enough to use the lessons one time with one class, whichever is less. Beyond that, rights must be purchased according to the appropriate category.

Application for Duplication Rights

The purchasing agency or individual must clearly specify the following:
1. Name, address, and telephone number
2. Titles of the books for Unlimited Duplication Rights contracts
3. Titles of activities for Unlimited Duplication Rights contracts
4. Names and addresses of school sites for which duplication rights are being purchased

NOTE: Books to be duplicated must be purchased separately and are not included in the contract for Unlimited Duplication Rights.

The requested duplication rights are automatically authorized when proper payment is received, although a *Certificate of Duplication Rights* will be issued when the application is processed.

Address all correspondence to:
Contract Division
AIMS Education Foundation
P.O. Box 8120
Fresno, CA 93747-8120